Dear Jane,

I enjoyed our discussion about the Hospital Council. Thanks again and I look forward to our future discussion.

Best regards

Gary Kaplan

EXECUTIVE GUIDE TO MANAGING DISPUTES

Executive Guide to Managing Disputes

Using ADR to Save Time and Expense
In Business, Healthcare and the Workplace

Gary L. Kaplan, Esq.

Beard Books
Washington, D.C.

Dedication

To Lori, Andrew and Sam
and
In loving memory of Sidney Kaplan

Contents

FOREWORD

In recent years, I litigated two cases that exemplify much of what is wrong with litigation. In both cases, my clients were businesses involved in commercial disputes involving more than $1 million. In both cases, my clients accepted sizable settlements in advance of final court decisions. In both cases, however, the settlements only marginally exceeded the costs of the lawsuits, which had been vigorously defended based on legal theories wholly at odds with the applicable law.

Why did these clients settle? First, the cost of completing a trial, and likely appeal, of these matters was likely to exceed the amounts that could be recovered. Second, the ability of the court to understand and fairly address complex legal and factual issues was in doubt.

These cases are far from unusual: it is well known that more than 95 percent of cases settle either before or during trial. The problem is that settlements are often reached after much, if not most, of the staggering costs of the litigation have been incurred. In some cases, there are substantial expenses in advance of settlement because the parties require significant discovery and key legal rulings to reach informed decisions about the settlement value of their cases. In other cases, settlements are unnecessarily delayed simply because of intransigence. In such cases, parties are willing to negotiate realistically and in good faith only after the cost and stress of litigation have beaten them down.

The shortcomings of litigation as a means of resolving business disputes are not limited to the cost of delayed settlements or even the cost of an increasingly rare trial. If the costs of litigation bore some reasonable relationship to the quality of the resulting decisions, those costs could be justified as necessary to the fair administration of justice. In this context, the quality of the decision made by a judge or jury can be measured not in terms of outcomes, but in terms of the reasoning and understanding that informed the decision. One would expect that a ruling by an impartial decision-maker based on a thorough understanding of the facts and applicable law would be more just (and of a higher quality) than one based on misunderstanding and personal biases. Unfortunately, experience suggests the opposite: there is often no correlation between the amount of money spent on litigation and the quality of the result.

The cost and inefficiency of litigation as a means of resolving disputes is well known. Other than aspersions cast on supposedly greedy lawyers, and complaints about the excesses of discovery, few explanations have been offered for the seeming disconnect between the expense of litigation and its sad performance in meting out justice.

In fact, the inadequacy of litigation as a means of resolving business disputes is systemic. The litigation process requires multiple iterations of redundant and time-consuming tasks by costly teams of professionals that often have little bearing on resolution of the subject disputes. Further, effective and zealous legal representation of a party to a complex business dispute is simply hard work, as it often requires sixty- or seventy-hour work for weeks on end.

I would like to thank Dr. Jane Siegel and Nick Frollini of Carnegie Mellon University, Professor Richard Bales of the Northern Kentucky University/Chase College of Law, and Professor Charles B. Craver of The George Washington University Law School for their generous and thoughtful comments on draft versions of this book.

Gary L. Kaplan

ABOUT THE AUTHOR

Gary L. Kaplan, Esq., has twenty-five years' experience addressing complex business disputes and transactions as a litigator, business counselor and dispute resolution professional. Mr. Kaplan is a graduate of Yale University (B.A. 1980, summa cum laude, distinction in economics) and the University of Chicago Law School. Based in Pittsburgh, Mr. Kaplan is a Partner in the law firm DeForest, Koscelnik, Yokitis, Kaplan and Berardinelli, and he is a member of the bars of California, the District of Columbia, Pennsylvania, Ohio, and West Virginia. As an arbitrator and mediator, Mr. Kaplan serves as a Neutral on panels of the American Arbitration Association, CPR Institute for Dispute Resolution, the American Health Lawyers Association, the National Arbitration Forum, and the U.S District Court for the Western District of Pennsylvania. Mr. Kaplan has written and spoken frequently on legal matters related to alternative dispute resolution, competition law, and information technology, and he teaches as a Professorial Lecturer in Law at the George Washington University Law School. He has also been listed for many years in the Best Lawyers in American and Who's Who in America Law. Additional information is available at www.managingdisputes.com, and Mr. Kaplan can be contacted at glkaplan@gmail.com.

CHAPTER I: The Executive's Guide to Litigation: What to Expect and Why Even Winners Lose

"May you have a lawsuit in which you know you are right."

—*A Gypsy Curse*

Although due process and public expectations mandate jury trials of criminal claims and important social matters, litigation has little to commend it as a means of resolving private business disputes—it is time-consuming and costly and provides little assurance of informed and well-reasoned decisions based on a thorough understanding of often complex matters. Rather than serve to fairly and efficiently resolve claims made in good faith, the courts too often serve as a battlefield in which the weapon of choice is the ability of one party to force the opposing party to incur extraordinary expense.

As the most common and default means of resolving business disputes in the United States, however, litigation is the benchmark for evaluating alternative approaches. Accordingly, this first chapter provides an overview of traditional business litigation and its costly procedures.

The Anatomy of a Lawsuit

Investigation and Pleadings

The starting point for any lawsuit is the filing and service of a "complaint" and summons. The summons, which must be served by formal procedures, provides the defendant with notice that he or she has been sued in a particular court. The complaint explains the basis for the plaintiff's claims. In response, the defendant must, within a specified period, file an "answer" or object to the complaint on legal grounds by filing a motion to dismiss or another procedural form.

The procedural rules governing claims in United States federal courts—the Federal Rules of Civil Procedure—state that the complaint generally need only provide the defendant with notice of the factual basis for the plaintiff's claims; detailed discussion of the governing legal theories is not required. Certain types of claims, however, such as those alleging fraud, must be pled with "specificity." In other words, more detail is required for such claims.

Litigation Time Line

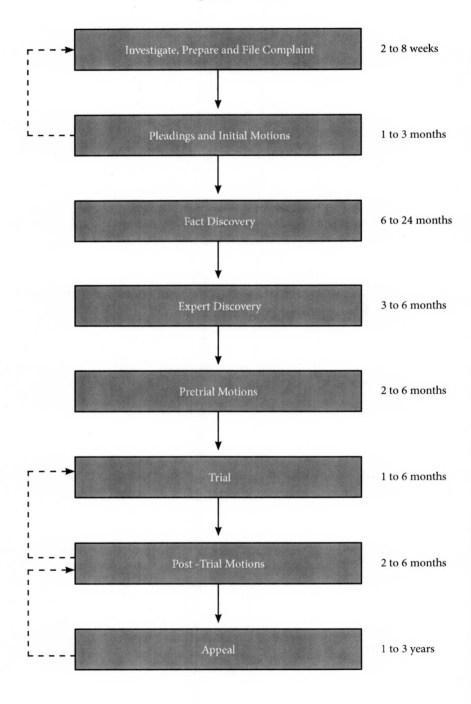

Notwithstanding the "notice pleading" framework of the federal rules, the mere initiation of a business lawsuit or a business defendant's initial response can cost tens of thousands of dollars. Before filing the complaint, legal counsel must first interview the client and relevant company personnel to learn the factual underpinnings of the dispute. Likewise, numerous relevant documents, emails and other materials may need to be considered. In addition, researching and reviewing the laws and legal standards likely to cover the plaintiff's claims becomes necessary. Once the foundation has been laid for the complaint, preparing and reviewing several drafts to ensure completeness and accuracy may also be necessary.

Such preparations are required for a few reasons. First, although the Federal Rules of Civil Procedure permit an action to be initiated with minimal details, as a practical matter the courts are reluctant to permit significant increases in the scope of an action when it nears its trial date. Second, as the reference document for the action, a poorly drafted complaint may impair a party's credibility and, therefore, his or her effectiveness in court.

Upon receipt of a complaint, the defendant's legal counsel must engage in reciprocal preparations. In many cases, it will be necessary or advisable to investigate and initiate counter claims as a means of putting the entire dispute before the court and/or to balance the strategic framework of the case.

Alternatively, the defendant's counsel may choose to challenge the plaintiff's complaint on legal grounds. For example, the defendant may argue that even if all of the facts alleged in the complaint are proved to be true, the plaintiff's claims could fail to state a valid cause of action under the applicable law. Or, the defendant may argue that the complaint fails to provide enough details about the alleged wrongdoing to allow for a proper response. In some cases, the defendant may argue that the plaintiff's claims are barred by a statute of limitations or that the plaintiff lacks standing to file the suit; *i.e.*, the plaintiff is not the proper party to be bringing the action.

Even if the defendant prevails in a legal challenge to a complaint, the action may not end there. In most cases, the court will permit the plaintiff to amend or revise a deficient complaint, thereby starting the pleading process over (and, of course, raising costs).

Preliminary Conference and Scheduling

Once the pleadings and/or initial motions are completed, most federal courts will call a preliminary conference to set the schedule for pretrial matters, such as discovery and post-discovery motions, and may set a preliminary date for trial. Recognizing that few cases proceed in accordance with their initial schedules, many courts simply schedule a date for a post-discovery conference, at which time the trial is scheduled.

Discovery

Litigation in the United States, in contrast to most other countries, is characterized by extensive and wide-reaching discovery in advance of trial. Except for privileged communications between attorneys and their clients, and materials prepared specifically for purposes of litigation, the parties in litigation can be compelled to produce every paper and electronic record in their possession and to provide multiple witnesses to testify in deposition, as long as the request for such information can be justified as either evidence for trial or information that may lead to the discovery of admissible evidence.

In theory, discovery is supposed to allow for a complete exposition of the facts to avoid surprises at trial. While discovery does promote such legitimate goals, it also imposes heavy and difficult-to-justify expenses on the parties. The cost of discovery entails not only the collection, review and production of massive amounts of information, but also the inevitable squabbles between the parties as to whether each has complied with his or her respective obligations.

Indeed, books on the theory and tactics of "effective" discovery could fill more than one library. Unfortunately, strategy often include tactics not only to assure thoroughness, but also to impede the opposing party's efforts.

For example, one party in litigation may produce a roomful of records to create the appearance of responsiveness to the other party's requests while manufacturing dubious pretexts for withholding the handful of records that really matter. Worse, the same tactic can be repeated over and over again in a single case.

Efforts to extract plainly relevant information in discovery may require multiple motions to the court. In response, counsel resisting discovery may contend that he or she has already produced thousands of pages of documents and should therefore not be obligated to produce additional (albeit, the relevant) documents. Remarkably, such patently absurd logic—in which the weight of documents is given priority over their content—is far from uncommon in litigation.

The federal courts have struggled with discovery abuses and costs for decades without much success. In the 1990s, they adopted a new rule requiring the parties to disclose relevant information voluntarily at the outset of a case. The Advisory Committee Notes to the new rule explain:

The rule requires all parties (1) early in the case to exchange information regarding potential witnesses, documentary evidence, damages, and insurance, (2) at an appropriate time during the discovery period to identify expert witnesses and provide a detailed written statement of the testimony that may be offered at trial through specially retained experts, and (3), as the trial date approaches, to identify the particular evidence that may be offered at trial. The enumeration in Rule 26(a) of items to be disclosed does not prevent a court from requiring by order or local rule that the parties disclose additional information without a discovery request. **Nor are parties precluded from using traditional discovery methods to obtain further information regarding these matters,** as for example asking an expert during a deposition about testimony given in other litigation beyond the four-year period specified in Rule 26(a)(2)(B).

A major purpose of the revision is to accelerate the exchange of basic information about the case and to eliminate the paper work involved in requesting such information, and the rule should be applied in a manner to achieve those objectives. (Emphasis added.)

Contrary to the objective of the new rule to reduce costs, it has simply added another step in the cumbersome process of going to trial. The fundamental problem with "initial disclosures" is that no litigator in his or her right mind will believe that the opposing party has in fact disclosed all of the relevant information in his or her possession. Consequently, the initial disclosures will inevitably be followed with the full panoply of discovery procedures.

Before the age of electronic records, email, and the Internet, discovery typically required parties to produce paper documents and deposition testimony from witnesses. Now, those traditional avenues of discovery have been supplemented (and overtaken) by discovery of electronic information.

In 2006, the federal courts adopted rules specifically directed at discovery of electronic records. Most significantly, those rules codified a principle stating that once a party has received notice that litigation may be initiated (either by or against that party), it must preserve all relevant information, including electronic documents. This requirement, for example, prohibits a business (or individual) from deleting emails in the ordinary course of its business so as to preserve electronic storage space. The new rules also address the cost of such discovery in providing that a party need not produce electronically stored information from sources that he or she identifies as "not reasonably accessible" because of undue burden or cost. If the opposing party files a motion to compel production of such information, the responding party bears the burden of establishing the undue burden or cost. Upon such a showing, the court may order discovery only for "good cause," for example, if the information is important to the case and not available from other sources.

Of course, as with other complex discovery issues, the cost of electronic discovery may be multiplied by the cost of disputes over what and how electronic information must be produced.

The advent and expansion of electronic discovery has not, of course, diminished traditional discovery procedures. Most notably, all material witnesses who are likely to testify at trial will probably be required to provide a preview of their expected testimony in a deposition. Depositions of important witnesses may be scheduled months or years in advance of the actual trial. In addition to witnesses with personal knowledge of the disputed events, depositions may be required to provide testimony with respect to a party's business practices, organization structures, and other matters that may provide guidance to more directly relevant information.

The cost of depositions is not limited to the expense of the court reporter and the time of attorneys eliciting testimony or representing the witness. The side requesting the deposition will first spend days reviewing documents to identify areas of inquiry during the deposition and to introduce as exhibits. In addition, counsel will probably prepare an outline and/or specific questions for the witness.

Meanwhile, the responding party will spend significant time reviewing the same documents to predict the questions to be asked at the deposition and, thereby, to assist the witness in preparing. The preparation of an important witness may require hours or days of what amounts to a rehearsal for the deposition.

Although ethical lawyers—the great majority—insist that their clients tell the truth during their depositions and testimony, witness preparation is intended to ensure that in responding to questions, the witness (a) frames responses in a manner that supports his or her party's positions and contradicts those of the opponent and/or (b) sheds as little light as possible on matters of interest to the opposing party's questioner. The simple fact is that there are many different truthful responses for most questions, and lawyers spend a great deal of time educating their clients on choosing the most favorable one.

Moreover, witness preparation is part of the tactical landscape of litigation. Litigation is far more about winning and losing than it is about obtaining a just resolution to a dispute. A key element of success in litigation is control of information: if one party has access to, and control over, more relevant information than the other party, his or her prospects for success at trial will be correspondingly greater. In view of this framework, each side hopes that its witnesses will disclose as little as possible to the other side during a deposition. The more helpful a witness is—in the form of providing detailed responses—to an opponent during a deposition, the greater the prospects for effective cross-examination at trial. In addition, a "helpful" deposition might make it less costly for the other party to complete discovery and otherwise prepare for trial. Meanwhile, expansive deposition testimony has no benefit to the party offering the testimony, because that party has the ability to discuss the case with its witnesses whenever necessary. For such reasons, litigators often advise their clients/witnesses to remember that although they can't win their case during their deposition, they can certainly lose it.

Expert Discovery

Many courts now distinguish between "expert" discovery (discovery of the opinions, qualifications and analyses of experts) and "fact" discovery (all other discovery). In some cases, the court will order expert discovery to be completed at the same time as fact discovery. In others, expert discovery is delayed until after completion of fact discovery. The timing depends primarily on whether the trial judge favors speed or thoroughness.

Expert discovery generally proceeds in two stages. First, the expert must prepare a written report for the court and the opposing party that summarizes his or her qualifications, analysis and opinions. The parties are also expected to produce in discovery all of the materials that the expert relied on in formulating his or her opinions. Second, the experts are deposed to allow for a fuller examination of their work on the case and to facilitate rebuttal testimony and cross-examination at trial.

The first approach of scheduling concurrent expert and fact discovery creates a significant risk of the expert discovery being costly and irrelevant. In complex business disputes, experts are frequently called upon to analyze, summarize and/or explain to the jury (and/or judge) the significance of evidence marshaled in fact discovery. If the expert is required to prepare reports before the completion of discovery, the report will, in many cases, be incomplete. In such cases, the expert may need to revise and/or amend his or her analysis and opinions for trial.

Changes to expert testimony during a case may raise concerns about the expert's credibility at trial and thereby weaken the claim or defense supported by such testimony. On the other hand, requiring premature reporting of expert opinions may effectively create a license for the experts to significantly revise and amend their opinions for trial. (Changes in testimony can be justified by simply explaining to the jury that not all of the relevant information was available at the time the report was required.) Such revisions, however, may make any intelligence garnered from the expert's report and deposition largely irrelevant and/or unhelpful for purposes of trial preparation.

The second approach to expert discovery poses a different problem. Simply by virtue of the delays between the preparation of the experts' reports, the experts' depositions and the trial, the experts may often be required to review the same materials many times. Unlike litigation counsel, experts are unlikely to be fully engaged in a particular dispute over its history. If the experts' reports and depositions and the trial are separated by months (or even years), they may need to redo much of their work for each step of the case simply to refresh their memories of the facts, issues and relevant analyses.

Notwithstanding the high cost of expert testimony in complex cases, the net effect of such efforts is not always clear. In complex cases, the subject matter—even with the benefit of expert testimony—may lie too far beyond the experience of the jury. In such cases, the jury may simply view one expert or the other as offering justification for deciding the matter based on personal biases.

Studies of juries and other decision makers (e.g., physicians) suggest that heuristics (or logical shortcuts) often play a prominent role in assessing complex issues. If a juror forms an initial impression of which side of the case he or she prefers or is biased against one side or the other, the juror will tend to look for (and rely on) evidence (such as expert testimony) that supports his or her preferred outcome—regardless of the merits of opposing views.

Alternatively, the opposing experts in a case may simply cancel each other out in the minds of the jury and add little to its assessments (either rational or irrational) of the merits of the case.

Pretrial Motions

While expenses related to fact and expert discovery have frequently been blamed for the high cost of business litigation, pretrial motions and other tactics can be equally, or more, costly.

Pretrial motions can serve a multitude of purposes. For example, motions may be filed (i) to seek delays or continuances; (ii) to address discovery disputes, *i.e.,* disputes over whether and how information must be disclosed; (iii) to seek summary judgment, *i.e.,* full or partial resolution of the case in advance of trial; (iv) to challenge the admissibility of expert testimony if, for example, the expert plans to testify about matters contrary to accepted principles in his or her field or employs unreliable analytic techniques; or (v) to limit the scope of evidence to be presented at trial; and so on.

In addition to serving their stated purposes, pretrial motions can be used to attempt to "educate" the judge about the case in advance of trial. As with experts and in contrast to litigation counsel, the trial judge is likely to devote only a small percentage of his or her time to any particular case in advance of trial and may have little understanding of the factual or legal issues in dispute. Consequently, motions provide an opportunity for the litigants to try to inform and persuade the court about key issues before going to trial. For example, a pretrial motion may try to lay the groundwork for favorable jury instructions. However helpful, pretrial motions are inevitably expensive.

Trial Preparation

After the completion of discovery, expert discovery and pretrial motions, and before the trial actually begins, a case enters an additional and intensive phase of preparatory work—final preparations for trial. In many respects, a trial is like a dramatic play put on by two competing groups of producers, directors and actors in the hope of getting the thumbs-up from the only critics that matter— the judge and/or jury. Therefore, the weeks (or even months) directly before trial typically require intensive effort to prepare and refine the "script" for trial and to set the stage.

The script will include opening statements, witness interrogations and closing statements to the jury. However, trial preparation, like a play, requires much more than the script—it requires coordinating evidentiary and demonstrative exhibits, proposed jury instruction, efforts to persuade the judge to adopt favorable legal interpretations, plans for selection of the jury, management and scheduling of fact and expert witnesses (which may require subpoenas), and all presentations to be made in court.

In view of the length of time between the facts giving rise to a lawsuit and the trial itself, it is often necessary to spend hours or days with important witnesses to refresh their recollections of key events and documents. In addition, rehearsals are needed to educate witnesses about what to expect at trial, including cross-examination, and to help them overcome their inevitable nervousness.

Also, litigation counsel must become familiar with, and plan for, the layout of the court in which the trial will take place. Some modern courtrooms are equipped with technology for displaying electronic exhibits, while others are not. In either case, plans for using courtroom technology must also be refined and rehearsed.

As with the production of any significant show or event, the final preparations may require several times the effort (and therefore expense) of the trial itself. A trial expected to last two weeks may easily require two months or more of intensive work leading up to it.

Jury Selection

In jury trials, the jury will typically be selected during the morning of the day scheduled for trial. Most jurors diligently attend to their responsibilities and follow the rules as dictated by the court. Unfortunately, the more complex (and therefore lengthy) the prospective trial, the less likely it is that the jury will be composed of individuals who have significant business or other experience that might be helpful in comprehending the business and technical issues raised in such cases. Although it is an oversimplification to say so, courts are rightly sympathetic to the demands facing professionals and businesspeople who simply cannot afford to miss work for weeks on end, so many qualified potential jurors are simply excused from lengthy trials.

Even assuming that a well-qualified jury is impaneled for a case, the litigants face a number of obstacles in winning their hearts and minds. First, most jurors prefer to be elsewhere—they have families, jobs, responsibilities and interests that must all be largely put on hold during the trial. Second, jurors may resent their complete lack of control over the events related to the trial. Third, and contrary to what is commonly shown on television and in the movies, long stretches of a trial may simply be boring or difficult to follow and may therefore be ignored by individual jurors.

In addition, many if not most of the rules that typically govern jurors' conduct during a trial make their jobs harder, if not impossible. For example, in many courts, jurors are confronted with some or all of the following restrictions:

- Jurors may not talk during the trial.
- Jurors may not take notes during the trial.
- Jurors may not discuss the case with one another during breaks.
- Jurors may not discuss the case at home.
- Jurors may not ask questions of the fact witnesses, experts or lawyers.
- Jurors may not take breaks unless ordered by the court.
- Jurors may not eat or drink in the jury box.
- Jurors may not receive phone calls.

Although these rules may have sound historical foundations, such as to prevent better note-takers from having undue influence in deliberations, they may prevent even the most diligent juror from focusing on and comprehending important elements of the trial.

A patent dispute, for example, might involve complex engineering or scientific concepts that require days of testimony to elucidate. In such a case, expecting a juror to comprehend and apply those concepts is like asking a college student to take an exam covering several weeks of a physics class after having been prohibited from taking notes or asking questions about the subject.

Trial

Once the trial begins, litigation counsel, support personnel and client personnel must devote themselves entirely to the case. Trials have been aptly described as battles between two warships, in which the combatants fight on the seas during the day and return to port each evening, where they must regroup, reload and plan for the next day's encounter. Since even the most complete preparations cannot predict the course of a trial with precision, both sides must be able to adapt and respond to unexpected developments as they arise.

In jury trials, because of the rules prohibiting interactions with jurors the parties' lawyers must guess at whether the jurors have been provided with sufficient background and explanatory information about complex issues to make informed decisions.

Alternatively, and not uncommonly, the lawyers will assume that the jurors will not understand the issues, so their presentations will be largely directed at aligning themselves with the presumed biases of the jurors—to the extent that they can be predicted—rather than at persuading jurors of the merits of their positions based on objective assessments of the applicable law.

The difference between what the law says and how jurors actually decide cases is a frequent subject in seminars and books on trial advocacy. For example, materials published by the National Institute for Trial Advocacy (NITA)—perhaps the leading educational organization directed at professional trial practice skills—explain:

> One of the most common mistakes made by inexperienced trial lawyers is to place too much emphasis on the legal elements of their claims and the proof required to satisfy those elements. It goes without saying that you will lose your case if you cannot prove the legal elements that make up your claims. In every case, therefore, you need to create some sort of matrix in which you connect the evidence you want to offer with the legal elements of all your claims or defenses. But juries do not necessarily go

into jury rooms with legal elements on their minds. They think in terms of basic fairness, not five-pronged legal tests. So give them what they want: a sense of fairness.

To understand how best to arrive at your fairness points for trial, you should set aside the legal elements of your claims or defenses for a moment and ask yourself these questions: Why is it fair for my client to win? Why would it be unfair for the other side to win? The answers to these questions have little to do with the elements of the claims or the instructions to the jury. The answers instead have everything to do with ordinary life experiences and ordinary conversations.[1]

The generally accepted fact that jurors decide cases based on "fairness" rather than on application of the law sounds sensible enough in the abstract. The problem, however, is that individual notions of fairness, when divorced from reasoned application of the law, depend on, and may be indistinct from, personal biases that have little or nothing to do with the merits of the case.

Thus, the NITA materials include the following examples of "fairness" points that might be made at trial. (PJR is the abbreviation for "possible juror reaction.")

- The only thing the defendant does is make this one product, and the entire future of the company depends on the success of that product.

  PJR: *I wouldn't want to do anything to completely shut down the defendant company. That would be pretty harsh. I hope we can resolve this case without destroying the company.*

- While my client worked seven days a week to help this company, the owners of the company, who are now suing my client, worked short hours and took long vacations. My clients are hardworking people with families.

  PJR: *I like hardworking people with families. They should get more of a break in life.*

- A judgment against my clients would ruin their business and force them to fire over fifty people.

  PJR: *I wouldn't want to be responsible for fifty people losing their jobs.*

---

[1] (Gross & Charles, 2003).

- All the executives at the defendant company will tell you that they are ashamed at how the company acted in this case.

  PJR: *If the higher-ups at the company think something is wrong with this deal, then something must be wrong.*

- A judgment against the defendant will be like a drop of water on a windshield: The company won't even notice it.

  PJR: *I'll sleep fine tonight if I rule against the defendant. It's no big deal.*[2]

In fact, trials commonly include more dramatic appeals to juror biases than the examples provided by NITA.

Moreover, in complex business disputes, the consequences of juror biases may be far more pronounced than in routine matters. If a juror doesn't understand the complex technical or legal issues that may lie at the heart of a dispute, he or she will inevitably make a decision based on more comfortable subjects, such as whether the plaintiff or defendant is personally sympathetic, appears friendlier, is more attractive and so on.

This aspect of litigation is perhaps the most ironic and troubling. After spending thousands, or even millions, of dollars in pleadings, discovery, motions and trial preparations, the ultimate success or failure of a party's claims or defenses in litigation may ultimately depend more on what kind of suit a key witness wore during the trial than on the substance of his or her testimony.

Post-Trial and Appeals

The cost of hard-fought litigation does not end at the conclusion of the trial, as the loser is unlikely to give up just because of an adverse verdict. Because a jury may decide the case based on irrelevant facts, or may simply make a mistake, the loser will inevitably hope for vindication on appeal before a more sanguine appellate court.

In the event of an appeal, litigation expenses may include the cost of briefs and preparation of the argument for the appeal as well as the expense of a completely new trial (if, for example, the appellate court determines that the trial was tainted by application of an improper legal standard) or further appeals to a higher court. Of course, if the case is remanded for a new trial, the losing party gets to start the entire costly process over again.

---

[2] (Ibid, pp. 31–32).

CHAPTER II: *The Persistence of Irrational Lawsuits*

"I was never ruined but twice: once when I lost a lawsuit and once when I won one."

– Voltaire

Litigation persists far longer and costs far more than would appear to be economically rational. This chapter discusses some of the reasons for this seeming anomaly.

The Honeymoon: In Love with Your Case

Each side begins litigation with visions of easy success. As the case drags on, the cost, stress, aversion to a trial and more realistic appraisals wear away at the parties' resolve. Ultimately, a settlement becomes each party's object of desire and hope. Most parties settle for the simple reason that the expense (and pain) of continuing eventually convinces the plaintiff that it is best to take less and the defendant to pay more than either would have considered at the outset of the case.

Given this well-established pattern, why is it so difficult for litigants to settle quickly and avoid the inevitable expense and stress? Classical economics suggests that financially rational litigants would recognize the pattern as well as the inevitable and unrecoverable monetary and personal costs of litigation and therefore work cooperatively to resolve their disputes as quickly, fairly and efficiently as possible.

Recent research now provides persuasive insight into why litigants are instead more likely to act against their own self-interest, *i.e.*, to act irrationally in economic terms, by persisting in a course of action whose costs far outweigh its benefits. Indeed, litigation is a perfect storm of psychological circumstances that conspire to prevent rational assessments of the strengths, weaknesses and values of claims and defenses, and to understate the time, cost and stress of the litigation itself.

Social scientists have identified, tested and explained a variety of human character traits, or biases, that are particularly relevant in litigation. These traits include the "self-serving" bias (*i.e.*, the tendency to evaluate facts in the light most favorable to oneself); the "confirmation" bias (*i.e.*, the tendency to filter and interpret new information in a manner that confirms one's own preconceptions or initial view); the "availability" bias (*i.e.*, the tendency to overstate the importance of available information); the "overconfidence" bias and illusions of control (*i.e.*, the tendency to overstate one's ability to affect outcomes); the "over-optimism" bias (*i.e.*, the tendency to understate the likelihood of bad outcomes); and attribution error (*i.e.*, the tendency to ascribe motives and intent erroneously to unfortunate circumstances).

While such biases may not apply in all instances and will affect parties to litigation (and their counsel) differently, taken together they help explain the unfortunate persistence of irrational litigation. Indeed, lawyers may be especially prone to such biases simply by virtue of their training and their duty to zealously protect their clients' interests.

Self-Serving Bias: Confusing Fairness with Self-Interest

"However top-lofty and idealistic a man may be, he can always rationalize his right to earn money."

–Raymond Chandler

Although litigants frequently profess to want only "justice" (and fair compensation if the plaintiff or vindication if the defendant), it is remarkable how both parties can invariably look at the same set of facts and reach remarkably different conclusions as to what "justice" requires. Moreover, research has persuasively shown that the parties' conflicting assessments of a case do not stem solely (or in some cases, at all) from disagreement over the facts giving rise to the dispute. Rather, once the parties have staked their claims, their respective views of "justice" are tainted by self-interest to a far greater extent than they are likely to realize or admit.

Two often-cited studies illustrate how one's team or position affects one's perspective. In a 1954 study,[3] students from Princeton and Dartmouth were asked to review a film of a football game between the two schools and to count the number of penalties by each side. The Princeton students found that the Dartmouth team committed twice as many flagrant penalties and three times as many mild penalties as the Princeton team. On the other hand, the Dartmouth students found that the two teams committed an approximately equal number of penalties. The study concluded that it was as though the two groups "saw a different game."

---

[3] (Hastorf & Cantril, 1954).

More relevant for present purposes, the "self-serving" bias was clearly demonstrated in a 1997 study by Professors George Lowenstein and Linda Babcock that considered how a group of "plaintiffs" and "defendants" evaluated a single hypothetical case.[4] Specifically, Lowenstein and Babcock asked college students who were divided into plaintiffs and defendants to evaluate a tort case in which an injured motorcyclist sued the driver of the car that collided with him for $100,000. All students were given the same twenty-seven-page case file and were then asked to predict how a judge would rule and the amount that a neutral third party would consider to be a fair settlement. The students were then given thirty minutes to negotiate a settlement and financial incentives to resolve the matter efficiently. (Specifically, the students, who were paid for the study, would be allocated payments based on the results of their settlement or the "court's" ruling. In the absence of a settlement, both parties would incur "court costs" that would reduce their payments.)

In the initial version of the study, the students were advised of their roles before reviewing the case file. The parties' self-serving biases were demonstrated in that the students assigned to the plaintiff's role predicted a judicial ruling that averaged $14,527 higher than students assigned to the defendant's role. Likewise, the student "plaintiffs" assessed the fair settlement value of the case $17,709 higher than student "defendants."

Next, Lowenstein and Babcock demonstrated that this bias was not simply a product of the students' assignment to a plaintiff or defendant role, but that it reflected their skewed interpretations of the case file. In a second round of the study, some students were assigned to a control group that was instructed to review and assess the case file before their designation as plaintiffs or defendants.

The second round confirmed that the students' assigned role affected how they first interpreted the case file: when they didn't know which roles they would be assigned until after they read the case and made assessments of the judge and fairness, the case "settled" 94 percent of the time. By contrast, when students knew what their roles would be before reviewing the file, only 72 percent of the cases settled.

Finally, Lowenstein and Babcock sought to identify methods for counteracting the self-serving bias. Simply by telling the students about the bias improved the accuracy with which they predicted the valuations of the case to be made by the opposing party (but did not induce them to make more accurate assessments themselves). If the students were told about the bias and then asked to write an essay in support of their opponent's position, the parties'

---

[4] (Babcock & Loewenstein, 1997).

biases actually increased—presumably because they led the students to reaffirm their commitments to their own positions. On the other hand, Lowenstein and Babcock were able to counteract the bias by advising the students of the bias and then instructing them to list the weaknesses in their own case. Under this approach, the difference between the plaintiff's and defendant's average assessment was reduced from $21,783 to only $4,674, and the rate of failed settlement negotiation declined from 35 percent to 4 percent.

Such research implies that initiating litigation is in itself likely to affect how each party considers the facts in dispute and to cause each side to interpret facts in the light most favorable to its position. Although it may be possible for a third party to intervene and counteract this bias, without a skilled mediator each party's bias will probably just help fuel the fire of litigation. Worse, the self-serving bias does not stand alone in promoting skewed perceptions and assessments of a dispute.

Confirmation Bias: Seeing What We Want to See

Closely related to the self-serving bias is the "confirmation" bias. Confirmation bias refers to our tendency to interpret new information in a manner that supports, and avoids contradicting, pre-existing beliefs. In other words, people see what they want to see. Tolstoy presaged the social-scientific study of this trait when he wrote: "I know that most men, including those at ease with problems of the greatest complexity, can seldom accept the simplest and most obvious truth if it be such as would oblige them to admit the falsity of conclusions which they have proudly taught to others, and which they have woven, thread by thread, into the fabrics of their life."[5]

One of Abraham Lincoln's most famous writings—his open letter responding to an editorial by Horace Greeley on July 19, 1862, that challenged Lincoln to declare his position on the emancipation of slaves—elicited strong public responses from both progressive abolitionists and conservative pro-unionists favoring appeasement of the secessionist states. Lincoln wrote:

Executive Mansion,
Washington, August 22, 1862.

Hon. Horace Greeley:
Dear Sir.

---

[5] (Tolstoy, 1897). *See also,* (Tolstoy, The Kingdom of God is Within You-Chapter III, 1893) ("The most difficult subjects can be explained to the most slow-witted man if he has not formed any idea of them already; but the simplest thing cannot be made clear to the most intelligent man if he is firmly persuaded that he knows already, without a shadow of doubt, what is laid before him.").

I have just read yours of the 19th. addressed to myself through the New-York Tribune. If there be in it any statements, or assumptions of fact, which I may know to be erroneous, I do not, now and here, controvert them. If there be in it any inferences which I may believe to be falsely drawn, I do not now and here, argue against them. If there be perceptable [sic] in it an impatient and dictatorial tone, I waive it in deference to an old friend, whose heart I have always supposed to be right.

As to the policy I "seem to be pursuing" as you say, I have not meant to leave any one in doubt.

I would save the Union. I would save it the shortest way under the Constitution. The sooner the national authority can be restored; the nearer the Union will be "the Union as it was." If there be those who would not save the Union, unless they could at the same time save slavery, I do not agree with them. If there be those who would not save the Union unless they could at the same time destroy slavery, I do not agree with them. My paramount object in this struggle is to save the Union, and is not either to save or to destroy slavery. If I could save the Union without freeing any slave I would do it, and if I could save it by freeing all the slaves I would do it; and if I could save it by freeing some and leaving others alone I would also do that. What I do about slavery, and the colored race, I do because I believe it helps to save the Union; and what I forbear, I forbear because I do not believe it would help to save the Union. I shall do less whenever I shall believe what I am doing hurts the cause, and I shall do more whenever I shall believe doing more will help the cause. I shall try to correct errors when shown to be errors; and I shall adopt new views so fast as they shall appear to be true views.

I have here stated my purpose according to my view of official duty; and I intend no modification of my oft-expressed personal wish that all men everywhere could be free.

Yours,
A. Lincoln.

Pulitzer prize-winning biographer Richard Carwardine explains that Lincoln's letter "[c]leverly... managed to reassure radicals that he was preparing for a dramatic step [of emancipation] and conservatives that he had no such intention."[6] Thus, Carwardine notes:

[Progressive] Sydney H. Gay of the *Tribune* happily reported a general impression that "you mean presently to announce that the destruction of Slavery is the price of our salvation." Yet [New York political figure] Thurlow Weed was sure that 'ultras' [*i.e.*, ultra-abolitionists] had taken a knock: 'They were getting the Administration into a false position. But it is all right now.' And Orville Browning now withdrawn into his conservative shell, told the president that he had 'reassured the country.'[7]

Early studies of the confirmation bias demonstrated people's tendency to examine only evidence supporting their theories or predictions while failing to consider contrary evidence. In 1960, cognitive psychologist Peter Cathcart Wason[8] presented test subjects with a three-number series—2, 4, 6—and told them that the series followed a specific rule that they could discover by testing their own three-number series. Every time the subject presented a three-number series to the experimenter, the subject was told whether the series satisfied or failed the rule. The subjects were also told that once they were sure that they discovered the rule, they should announce it to the experimenter.

Wason's study showed that once a subject identified a probable "rule," he or she tended to consider only evidence supporting his or her analysis. Although the actual rule was simply "any ascending sequence," the subjects often announced rules that were far more complex. Notably, the subjects seemed to test only "positive" examples—series that they believed would conform to their rule and confirm their hypothesis. On the other hand, they did not attempt to challenge or falsify their hypotheses by testing series that would violate their posited rules. Wason described this phenomenon as confirmation bias, whereby subjects systematically seek only evidence that confirms their hypotheses.

Regrettably, litigation provides ample opportunity for parties and their counsel to fall into the confirmation bias trap. For example, litigation attorneys may focus their discovery efforts on eliciting information that supports their case while failing to pursue contrary evidence. Moreover, this practice may facilitate irrational overconfidence.[9]

Perhaps more significantly, the confirmation bias can lead parties in litigation faced with ambiguous evidence to become more entrenched and

---

[6] (Carwardine, 2006).

[7] Ibid.

[8] (Wason, 1960).

[9] (Birke & Fox, 1999).

polarized in their positions. For example, two groups of students—twenty-four who favored capital punishment and believed that research supported the view that it served as a deterrent, and an equal number who opposed it and believed that research showed its inefficacy as a deterrent—were asked to evaluate various studies on the deterrent efficacy of the death penalty and to state whether a given study (along with criticisms of that study) provided evidence for or against the deterrence hypothesis. Subjects were then asked to rate the extent that the reference materials changed their attitudes toward the death penalty and their views on its efficacy as a deterrent.

The study showed that research materials served to polarize the students' opinions. Students who favored capital punishment and believed it served as a deterrent at the outset of the study reported a strengthening of their views as a result of the material. Meanwhile, students who opposed capital punishment and believed it to be ineffective as a deterrent at the outset of the study reported a strengthening of their contrary views.[10]

Similar results were obtained in a study examining the view of advocates and opponents of nuclear energy. The subjects of the study were provided identical information and arguments about the Three Mile Island nuclear disaster and a false military alert that could have resulted in a U.S. nuclear attack. After reading the reference materials, 54 percent of the subjects who supported the use of nuclear power viewed it more favorably, while only 7 percent viewed it less favorably. Meanwhile, 45 percent of the subjects who opposed the use of nuclear energy viewed it less favorably, while only 7 percent viewed it more favorably.[11]

Litigation is replete with opportunities for ambiguous information to polarize positions. Both discovery and court rulings can provide fodder for parties' conflicting assessments. In one of my recent cases, the parties participated in court-ordered mediation in advance of discovery, which proved unsuccessful. Two years later, after voluminous discovery and a court ruling that denied both parties' motions for summary judgment, the parties agreed again to seek a settlement through mediation. In denying both parties' motions, the judge had made a number of important legal rulings that we believed made the defendant's case untenable. We agreed to renew settlement discussions (in mediation) because we believed that our opponents would now see the error of their ways and approach the discussion more realistically than they had at the outset. Unfortunately, our opponents apparently held exactly the opposite

---

[10] (Lord, Ross, & Lepper, 1979).
[11] (Plous, 1991).

views of the court's rulings, and the renewed settlement discussions were even less productive than the efforts two years earlier.[12]

Availability: "What We Don't Know (or Understand) Can't Hurt Us"

In addition to the distortions caused by egocentric perceptions of fairness, parties to litigation may overstate their prospects for success at the outset of a case simply because they do not have all the facts. Often, parties to a dispute will be aware of only part of the relevant circumstances giving rise to a dispute. Unfortunately, the lack of complete information rarely serves as an impediment to wasteful litigation and may, in fact, encourage it.

Research has shown that individuals faced with uncertainty or incomplete information will selectively fill in details in ways that may promote conflict. First, both sides are likely to give more weight to the facts that they know or that easily come to mind than to hold a rational view of what all the relevant facts suggest is merited. This has trait been called the "availability heuristic." (A "heuristic" is a mental shortcut used to evaluate complex sets of facts.)

The forcefulness of the availability heuristic is shown by undue reliance on anecdotal evidence or past instances of a particular event and outcome; *i.e.,* reliance on the erroneous belief that "because it happened before it will happen again."

In research studies, the availability heuristic has been shown to apply not only to incomplete information (such as when a party knows only half of the relevant events), but also to more easily understood or accessible information. For example, psychologists Daniel Kahneman and Amos Tversky, who wrote the seminal work on this topic,[13] asked participants in a study to estimate the number of words that begin with the letter "R" or "K" in comparison to words that have the letter "R" or "K" in the third-letter position. Because it is far easier to recall words that begin with "R" (rooster, roar, rusty, red) or "K" (key, kitchen, kite) than words having "R" or "K" in the third-letter position (street, stream, ink, acknowledge), 66 percent concluded that words that begin with "R" or "K" are more common. The reality is that words that have the letter "R" or "K" in the third position are far more common than those beginning with those letters.[14]

A more common example is to ask study participants whether more people die in airplane crashes or car accidents. Because airplane crashes receive far more media attention, many people erroneously believe that they are responsible

---

[12] Ultimately, the case settled shortly before trial.
[13] (Tversky & Kahneman, 1974).
[14] (Kahneman & Tversky, 1982).

for more deaths, although statistics show that car crashes are responsible for far more fatalities.

In connection with litigation, availability biases can create irrational projection as to the benefits of litigation and to its costs. As noted above, at the outset of a case, each side may give undue weight to readily accessible facts while ignoring the implications of the full picture. In addition, parties are likely to underestimate the costs and stresses associated with litigation, because such negative consequences are remote from factors most commonly considered at the outset of a case—namely, the prospects for success or failure and the probable damage recoveries. As the trial approaches and the unpleasant prospect of spending weeks, or even months, in court becomes more "real," such negatives become more immediate and apparent, which may contribute to the high rate of settlement "on the courthouse steps."

Attribution Error: Assuming the Worst of the Opposition

It is worth noting that incomplete information often causes parties to a dispute to assume the worst about their opponents—that they intentionally acted with evil motives (and therefore should be punished). This issue, called attribution error, refers to the tendency of people to overemphasize (or project) personal characteristics contributing to an event, while minimizing circumstantial causes.[15] For example, the failure of an acquaintance to say hello when passing on the street may lead a person to conclude that the acquaintance is unfriendly and not to consider the possibility that the acquaintance was simply preoccupied and unaware of the other person.

Overconfidence, Undue Optimism and Illusions of Control

Finally, and perhaps most significantly, parties to litigation and their lawyers not only perceive facts and issues in the light most favorable to themselves, they also make unduly optimistic predictions about the duration, cost and effectiveness of their litigation efforts while minimizing those of their opponents.

There is a perennial debate among lawyers, judges and clients as to whether (or how often and to what extent) lawyers make a difference in the outcome of disputes. There will, of course, be some instances in which the legal talents of the opposing parties are so unevenly matched as to make the legal battle an unfair fight. However, such cases are likely to be in the great minority— particularly with respect to business disputes, in which each side will probably be represented by capable legal counsel. Although rigorous scientific analysis of this question is unlikely (because of the difficulty of designing a meaningful

---

[15] (Ross, 1977).

study), anecdotal evidence and survey research suggest that lawyers in complex cases, like experts, tend to balance each other out.[16]

Of course, no litigator is apt to admit that his or her client can expect only "average" results. Just as, according to Garrison Keillor, all of the children of Lake Wobegon are "above average," there can be little doubt that virtually all litigators would not only characterize themselves as "above average" but would also be insulted at the suggestion that they fall anywhere below the top 10 percent of their peers.

Self-deceptive overconfidence is not unique to lawyers; it is endemic to human nature. One study found that fully 94 percent of university professors believe that they do a better job than their colleagues.[17] Similarly, most people think that they are more intelligent and fair-minded than average.[18]

Overconfidence may be closely related to irrational forces affecting decision-making: individuals often believe that they have more control over outcomes than is possible. Perhaps the best example of this phenomenon is the New Jersey lottery. The lottery was a failure when ticket purchasers were given computer-selected numbers; it became a huge success when it was revised to permit purchasers to select their own numbers—even though the odds of winning were the same in either case.

Similarly, attorneys and their clients—like people in other circumstances—are prone to vastly overestimate the likelihood of positive outcomes and underestimate the likelihood of negative ones. In a seminal study, college students rated themselves much less likely than their peers to suffer from a drinking problem, have a heart attack, be fired from a job or divorce a few years after getting married.[19] Similarly, one review of the academic literature revealed the following:

- Second-year M.B.A. students overestimated the number of job offers they would receive and their starting salaries.
- Students overestimated the scores they would achieve on exams.
- Almost all the newlyweds in a U.S. study expected their marriages to last a lifetime, even while aware of the divorce statistics.

---

[16] (Kalven Jr. & Zeisel, 1966)(Citing judicial assessment to conclude that the quality of legal counsel is balanced in most cases); (Seidman Diamond, Casper, Heiert, & Marshall, 1996)("In sum, our data suggest that during deliberations jurors do not spend very much time discussing the attorneys who argued the case. Moreover, when they do talk about the attorneys their comments tend to deal with substantive points rather than personal attributes of or juror reactions to the attorneys themselves.").

[17] (Cross, 1999).

[18] (Birke & Fox, 1999, p. 7).

[19] (Weinstein, 1980).

- Professional financial analysts consistently overestimated corporate earnings.
- Most smokers believe they are less at risk of developing smoking-related diseases than others who smoke.[20]

Not surprisingly, similar findings of overoptimism were found in studies of trial lawyers. The authors of one study, for example, concluded that "lawyers tended to be overconfident in general, but especially so in cases in which they initially made highly confident predictions."[21]

Overoptimism with respect to an impending dispute is neither limited to, nor most dramatically illustrated by, litigation. Instead, the history of war is replete with poor, if not catastrophic, decisions based on misguided optimism. In February 2003, U.S. Secretary of Defense Rumsfeld confidently predicted that war in Iraq would be quickly over, when he told US troops in Aviano, Italy, "It is unknowable how long that conflict will last. It could last six days, six weeks. I doubt six months."[22] And on May 1, 2003, President Bush forever changed the perception of the phrase "Mission Accomplished" when he declared on the deck of the USS Abraham Lincoln that "[m]ajor combat operations in Iraq have ended."[23]

The Bush Administration hardly stands alone in the annuls of disastrous war predictions. Barbara W. Tuchman describes the epidemic of overoptimism that infected war plans leading to World War I:

The Germans... expected a short war...[that] would be over in four months.... "You will be home before the leaves have fallen from the trees," the Kaiser told departing troups in the first week of August... Count Oppersdorf ...said things could not last ten weeks; Count Hochberg thought eight weeks....

* * *

In St. Petersburg the question was not whether the Russians could win but whether it would take them two months or three months....The French gambling on a quick finish, risked no troups on what would have been a difficult defense of the Lorraine iron basin...As a result they lost 80 percent of their iron ore for the duration; and almost lost the war. The English, in

---

[20] (Armor & Taylor, 2002).
[21] (Loftus & Wagenaar, 1988).
[22] (Transcript of Town Hall Meeting At Aviano Air Base, 2003).
[23] (President Bush Announces Major Combat Operations in Iraq Have Ended , 2003).

their imprecise manner, counted vaguely on victory, without specifying when, where, or how, within a matter of months.[24]

Although of far less consequence, litigation similarly invites such extreme overconfidence. As shown in reports of contested legal fees, litigation costs can rise to two, three or more times initial estimates.

Further, overoptimism can persist in litigation even until the eve of trial. A recent study looked at trials that followed public offers of settlement under California's Rules of Civil Procedure.[25] Under California Rule 998, a party can publicly offer a settlement in advance of trial. If the opposing party rejects the offer and does not obtain a more favorable ruling at trial, then the party that rejected must bear certain of the offering parties' litigation costs. In other words, a rejection of a public settlement offer under Rule 998 implies that the party expects to receive a larger recovery at trial than has been offered in settlement.

Reaffirming the overoptimism bias, plaintiffs in the study erroneously concluded that trial was a superior option in 61.2 percent of the primary set cases, while defendants erred 24.3 percent of the time. Although plaintiffs made the wrong decision more frequently, the defendants' decisions were more costly. On average, plaintiffs who made the wrong decision lost $43,000 relative to the amount offered in settlement. By contrast, a wrong decision cost defendants, on average, $1,140,000.[26]

Conflicting Risk Profiles

Studies in both litigation and other fields have shown that people are more averse to taking a risk when they expect a gain, and more willing to take a risk when they expect a loss.[27] Professor Martin A. Asher explained to the New York Times:

If you a approach a class of students and say, 'I'll either write you a check for $200, or we can flip a coin and I will pay you nothing for $500,' most students till take the $200 rather than risk getting nothing." But reverse the situation, so that students have to write the check, and they will choose to flip the coin, risking a bigger loss because they hope to pay nothing at all, he continued. "They'll take the gamble."[28]

Assuming that the different roles of plaintiffs and defendants lead to such different risk profiles, risk-averse plaintiffs (who stand to gain in litigation)

---

[24] (Tuchman, 1994).

[25] (Kiser, Asher, & McShane, 2008).

[26] Ibid.

[27] (Gross & Syverud, 1996); (Rachlinski, 1996).

[28] (Glater, 2008)

may accept settlements even when their expected recovery at trial would be greater, but risk-seeking defendants (who stand to lose in litigation) may reject settlements matching expected payments at trial in hopes of avoiding payment altogether. Perhaps more importantly, a defendant's inclination to gamble on a complete victory may induce them to make unrealistically low offers or none at all, despite mounting costs for the litigation itself.

Wishful thinking, in its various guises, distorts not only positive perspectives about one's own case and ability to influence its outcome but also the effectiveness of one's adversaries. Litigants are prone to underestimate their opposition in two areas. First, and perhaps as a function of tendencies to view facts in a biased light, it is easy to underestimate the legitimate arguments and tactics that will be employed by the opposing party and its counsel. Thus, the cost and duration of the case may be multiplied as the result of legitimate disputes over discovery, pretrial motions, unanticipated discovery demands and third-party discovery and the like.

Second, and unfortunately, litigation is often characterized by illegitimate tactics, arguments and lies that can inflate costs considerably. The problem is that it is far easier and cheaper to make false and misleading arguments than to rebut them—especially when a case concerns complex subjects about which the judge or jury may have little if any knowledge or experience.

For example, a party may quote a single passage of a court decision out of context to support a legal argument, even though the decision—taken as a whole—contradicts the argument. In response, the opposing party will need to explain not only that the quotation was taken out of context but also provide the necessary context through a detailed discussion of the court decision in question. Indeed, litigation attorneys may be especially adept at distorting the factual record—through manipulation of context—to suit their clients' positions. In short, they are good at lying and in justifying their lies on the basis of their professional duties to their clients. This is, perhaps, a major reason for the low esteem to which trial lawyers are often held.

Married to Your Case with No Way Out

Irrational litigation persists not only because the parties appraise their cases unrealistically from the start but also because, once started, litigation is difficult to stop.

Part of the difficulty in halting even ill-considered litigation stems from the cost of litigation itself: the further a case progresses, the more it costs, with the parties' investment in the case contributing to intransigence.

Psychologist and behavioral economists refer to this issue as the "sunk cost" bias or "sunk cost" fallacy. In economic terms, "sunk costs" or "fixed costs" refer to investments that have been made but cannot be directly recovered through future actions, regardless of the success or failure of those actions. For example, if you buy a nonrefundable airline ticket to visit your aunt Mabel, you will not be refunded the cost of the ticket if you cancel the visit. Consequently, after the ticket has been paid for, its cost, according to economic theory, should be irrelevant to the decision of whether or not to go ahead with the trip. If you have a fight with Aunt Mabel and don't want to go, the fact that you paid $1,000 for the ticket should have no bearing on your decision, since you will not get the money back in any event.

Common experience (confirmed by research) shows, however, that people often cannot bring themselves to ignore sunk costs when deciding future actions and will, in fact, throw good money after bad to justify their prior mistakes. Part of the problem is analogous to the self-interest bias: once a party has spent money on a case, the investment itself is likely to taint his or her appraisal of the outcome. One study of this issue was made at a racetrack—bettors on a horse race were asked to predict their horse's chance of winning both before and after having made a bet. Of the 141 people asked, 72 had just placed a $2 bet within the past thirty seconds, and 69 were about to place a $2 bet in the next thirty seconds. On a scale of 1 to 7, with 7 referring to a sure winner, the people about to place a bet averaged a 3.48 rating of their chances for success (or a "fair chance of winning"), but people who had just finished betting averaged a 4.81 rating (or "good chance of winning").[29]

Further, people have a hard time admitting that they made a mistake. In another study, 96 business students were divided into two groups: half were told that, as a manager, they had made a bad R&D investment in an underperforming division of a company, while the other half were told that the former manager of the division had made the bad R&D investment. In both cases, the students were then asked to make a new $20 million investment (to be divided between the underperforming division and another division). The students "responsible" for the poor performance of the division were much more prone to invest in that division than the nonresponsible students. On average, the "responsible" students chose to invest $12.97 million, while the others only $9.43 million.[30]

Bad cases are also difficult to bring to a halt simply because cessation might invite retaliation and penalties. Under the Federal Rules of Civil Procedure, it

---

[29] (Knox & Inkster, 1969). See also (Arkes & Blumer, 1985); (Arkes & Hutzel, The Role of Probability of Success Estimates in the Sunk Cost Effect, 2000).

[30] (Staw, 1976). See also (Whyte, 1986).

is entirely proper to initiate litigation based on a good-faith belief in a cause of action and to rely on discovery to provide the necessary factual support. If, however, discovery does not bear out an asserted claim, it is highly unlikely that the plaintiff will walk away. In view of the sunk investments in the case, the plaintiff may opt to hope that the jury will make a mistake in his or her favor. In addition, the plaintiff may be reasonably concerned that conceding the invalidity of a claim would simply invite retaliation in the form of a claim alleging abuse of process, bad faith, etc., and prolong the matter in any event.

Conclusion

Notwithstanding the near certainty that litigation will be resolved in advance of trial, a host of human biases and predictable circumstances conspire to inflate both the cost and duration of lawsuits. As discussed in the next chapter, the inherent inefficiency of litigation as a process for making decisions on complex matters, magnifies the problem.

CHAPTER III: *The Litigation Problem: An Inefficient Process for Deciding Disputes*

Even if parties to litigation act entirely in accord with economic rationality, fairly value their claims and defenses, and pursue only valid legal theories in good faith and in accordance with the highest standard of ethics, they will suffer the consequences of a litigation system that is intrinsically inefficient, wasteful, and—in many instances—unlikely to produce a just resolution. Although it is easy, and commonplace, to blame lawyers for the high cost and general inefficiency of litigation as a means for resolving disputes, it is far more accurate to blame the litigation process itself. Litigation inherently encourages, if not demands, extraordinarily costly and wasteful expenditures of time and money, while offering few assurances that it will lead to a well-reasoned and just decision by a qualified, invested, and informed adjudicator.

Imagine that you are CEO of a computer company with two divisions that operate independently—a hardware division and a software division. Further, assume that your company has just been hit with an unexpected tax bill of $2 million, and the only way to make payment is to cut the budget of either the hardware or the software division. How do you go about deciding?

One possible approach is to let the divisions fight it out. Each division could hire a team of business consultants to explain why the other division should be cut. Because each division has only limited information about the other division, they each want access to each other's financial and technical information. Because of their desire to outdo each other, the division heads then fight with each other about the information they need, and request you, the CEO, to intervene from time to time.

Now, further assume that you do not want to decide the matter yourself, because you are afraid of the strife that your decision would create. Rather than hire a third consultant, you decide to let your accountant review each division's argument (and consulting report) and decide the matter. Although your accountant is very busy and has no expertise in hardware or software, you think she is fair and will do her best.

Would any rational business person decide how to pay an unexpected tax bill (or other liability) with such a method? Of course not. An adversarial approach to decision making generates duplicative consulting costs and wasteful battles over whether or not to share information. Further, by appointing a busy professional without relevant expertise to decide the matter, the likelihood of an optimal final determination is low.

Despite such inefficiencies and waste, the suggested approach is precisely how litigation operates as a method for resolving business and other civil disputes. The extraordinary costs of resolving business disputes may, on one hand, prevent businesses from even seeking resolution of just claims and, on the other, compel sizable settlement payments simply to prevent even greater litigation expenses. To make matters worse, the high cost of litigation neither assures nor promotes informed and well-reasoned decisions by qualified decision makers.

The shortcomings of litigation are most apparent when it is evaluated as a decision-making process for businesses in conflict that need to choose (or need to have some third party choose) among alternatives for allocating liabilities and losses between them. Within this framework, litigation can be evaluated like any other decision-making process in terms of the cost and the quality of the resulting decisions. Assuming that the goal of an efficient decision-making process is to make the best decisions at the lowest possible cost, it is doubtful that litigation exemplifies an optimal, or even reasonably efficient, process.

The Characteristics of Efficient Dispute Resolution

According to Adam Smith and subsequent generations of economists, markets (and competitors) operate efficiently because efficiency is rewarded and inefficiency is punished. In perfectly competitive markets (*i.e.*, markets that include numerous competitors selling undifferentiated products), the price of goods will stabilize at a level equal to the marginal cost of production of those goods (including a reasonable return on investment) because, on one hand, a competitor that prices above marginal cost (*i.e.*, the "equilibrium" or "market" price) will lose its customers to competitors charging the market price. On the other hand, a competitor seeking to increase its customer base by charging less than marginal cost will never be able to recoup the resulting loses on every good sold (and will ultimately go out of business). Although there are, of course, no perfectly competitive markets, Adams Smith's insight that competitive markets are characterized by economic incentives that promote efficiency provides guidance for examining systems and/or methods for resolving disputes.

Of course, before the efficiency of any system or process can be evaluated its objective(s) must be understood. In economic markets, for example, classical economics provides that resources are allocated efficiently (*i.e.*, to their best uses at the lowest cost) when the market price of a good equals its marginal cost of production. Efficiency in the context of dispute resolution, however, is more problematic because the goal of dispute resolution—whether called justice, fairness, or equity—cannot be directly quantified or measured. (Indeed, the subjective nature of justice or fairness contributes to the cost of efforts to resolve disputes.)

Although it may be impossible to translate justice or fairness into measurable commodities for purposes of economic analysis, the efficiency and quality of dispute resolution systems can be evaluated based upon some general principles and reasonable proxies for those goals.

First, uncoerced and consensual settlement agreements are preferred over decisions imposed by third parties. If fairness lies in the eye of the beholder, it is hard to argue against uncoerced consensual settlements of disputes. This does not mean that settlements are preferred at any price. A litigation settlement that stems from a party's fear over his or her ability to pay legal fees and court costs hardly qualifies as uncoerced. Similarly, a settlement induced with lies and/or the withholding of material information is not considered consensual.

Second, the quality of a resolution imposed by a decision maker (such as a judge, a jury or a neutral third party) depends on (i) the qualifications of the decision maker in terms of his or her education, training, and experience; (ii) the quality of the information provided to the decision maker; and (iii) the decision maker's investment of time and effort to understand and decide the dispute. In other words, when it is necessary for a third party to decide a dispute, the dispute resolution process should promote informed decisions by well-qualified and invested decision makers.

Third, other things being equal, less costly dispute resolution procedures are preferred over more costly ones. This principal simply acknowledges the potential trade-off between costs and quality of dispute resolution (or the decision-making process). Although every dispute between two parties could, in theory, be resolved at no cost by flipping a coin, such a mechanism would not assure or promote confidence in the fairness of the ultimate resolution.

As the primary method of formal dispute resolution in the United States, litigation is by necessity the benchmark against which other dispute resolution methods are evaluated. By any measure, the cost of modern litigation is extraordinary. It has been estimated that patent disputes now cost, on average, over $4 million to bring to trial. Although cost data for most litigation are unavailable, in business disputes, legal fees for each side commonly exceed $250,000. Indeed, the ability of a party to impose costs on other parties often serves as the main basis for settlement, rather than any criteria related to the merits of the dispute.

As a benchmark for dispute resolution methods, litigation has unfortunately become the paradigm of inefficiency (and often injustice) rather than a model to be emulated. As discussed below, the inefficiency of litigation cannot be attributed to malfeasance or greed of any group (*i.e.*, lawyers) but is instead systemic. Litigation today is no more efficient as a method for resolving complex modern disputes than is a bucket brigade—however well intentioned its members—for saving a modern high-rise from fire.

Indeed, and unfortunately, identifying the failings of litigation as a means for resolving private disputes fairly and efficiently is far easier than identifying its successes. In particular, litigation's inefficiency, as discussed below, is inevitable in view of its dependence on (i) wasteful redundancy, (ii) misdirected incentives, (iii) delayed rule-setting, and (iv) passive fact-finding.

Of course, the cost of litigation would be justified if it resulted in higher quality decision making and/or better served societal interests compared with other dispute methods. Unfortunately, the quality of decision-making in litigation often seems entirely unrelated to its costs. Further, societal benefits of judicial (as opposed to private) decision making in private disputes must be measured against the societal costs of clogged courts that are diverted from matters to which they are uniquely suited—serving as a check on abuses of legislative and/ or executive power, criminal matters, matters requiring clarifications of law, and other matters in which societal concerns may outweigh individual private interests.

Wasteful Redundancy

Before addressing concerns about the quality of decision-making in litigation (based upon the criteria discussed above), it is important to understand the key cost factors in litigation. The easiest, and most common, target for concerns about the cost of modern litigation is discovery. A common complaint is that discovery—the exchange of information between the parties in advance of trial through disclosure of documents, depositions, and written interrogatories— often accounts for 50 to 80 percent of litigation costs. However, identifying discovery as the cause of inflated litigation costs seems to misdiagnose a symptom of the problem as the problem itself.

Litigation is excessively costly not because of discovery, or even because it requires the services of qualified, and often costly, legal professionals. Litigation is too costly because it *requires* competing teams of lawyers to replicate each other's efforts in conducting discovery and performing a series of repetitive and redundant tasks.

The extraordinary duplication of efforts in business litigation arises from both the competition between the opposing sides and the process itself. Thus, in preparing for a trial, both (or all) sides of a case must review the same documents, interview the same witnesses, and attend the same depositions and hearings. Likewise, the opposing lawyers must examine the same body of relevant law and prepare for trial.

The inefficiency of litigation, moreover, does not end with discovery. Not only must the competing sides collect the same information in discovery, both must then prepare their competing but inherently overlapping presentations of those facts for trial. Meanwhile, testimony taken from adverse witnesses in depositions and friendly witnesses in interviews must be elicited and reproduced at trial.

In many respects, a trial can be considered a documentary play about an event or series of events. To prepare for trial, each party must investigate and analyze the facts of the conflict and present them in context based upon the applicable law. The presentation of evidence to the judge and/or jury then follows a script carefully crafted by each party's attorney to emphasize favorable and/or dramatic circumstances. Moreover, the trial often follows weeks of rehearsal by attorneys and witnesses to assure that they follow the designated script. The main differences between a trial and a literary drama is that, in litigation, each party must draft its own script based largely on the same facts and law and then they must argue about which script is more accurate.[31]

The Invisible Hand Gone Awry: Incentives That Promote Inefficiency

The second characteristic of litigation that often drives up costs is that, on one hand, the process is largely devoid of economic incentives that promote efficiency (at least in the short run) and, on the other hand, is replete with incentives to act inefficiently.

First, unlike most projects, litigation has no objective benchmarks (other than the passage of time) that allow clients to determine when the work, such as preparation for trial, is complete. In construction, the client can track expenses against progress toward completion. In information technology, software under development either meets its specifications or does not. By contrast, the only benchmark for trial preparation is the litigator's own assessment of the amount

---

[31] Of course, in litigation the parties not only get to present their own scripts, they also get to criticize (*i.e.*, cross-examine) the scripts of the other parties. Such cross-examination often sheds light on biases, omissions, and even falsehoods of the competing parties' scripts. For this reason, cross-examination is considered a fundamental tenet of due process.

of discovery, briefing, and witness preparation necessary to his or case.   In assessing the required level of preparation, however, several interrelated factors conspire to promote excess rather than moderation and efficiency, including hourly rates, competition (*i.e.*, concerns about keeping up with the other side), the risk of malpractice claims, and uncertainty.

Hourly Rates

The most obvious incentive contrary to efficiency in litigation is created by the manner in which attorneys are paid.   This creates what economists call an "agency problem"—which means that an agent's incentives, in this case, an attorney in litigation, are not fully aligned with those of the principal or client. Obviously, clients want disputes to be resolved with as little cost as possible. Regardless of whether a client stands to win or lose in litigation, his or her costs for the litigation are generally an unrecoverable loss.[32] By contrast, the lawyer's recovery (when paid hourly) increases as the duration and costs of the case increase.   Consequently, given a choice between settling a case for $100,000 at the outset or for the same $100,000 immediately before trial, the client will prefer the former, while his or her lawyer will have strong incentive to favor the latter.

Professors Robert Mnookin and Lee Ross offer an especially cynical view of the implications of the divergent incentives of lawyers and their clients:

> Litigation is fraught with such principal/agent problems. In civil litigation
> for example—particularly where lawyers on both sides are being paid
> by the hour—there is very little incentive for the opposing lawyers to
> cooperate.   Indeed, the incentive structure may induce them to favor
> costly, noncooperative litigation.   This may be particularly true if the
> clients have capacity to pay for trench warfare and derive satisfaction from
> the costs they impose on the other side. ...Commentators have suggested
> that ... so many cases settle on the courthouse steps, and not before. Such
> a late settlement allows attorneys to avoid the possible embarrassment of
> an extreme and unfavorable outcome, while at the same time providing

---

[32] Under the "American Rule," the plaintiffs and defendants in litigation are typically responsible for their litigation costs, regardless of which party ultimately prevails. Although statute creates exceptions to this rule for certain types of claims, the majority of cases in the United States follow this rule. Under the "British Rule," the losing party is responsible for the winning party's costs and legal fees. Although the British and American Rules may affect the parties' incentives to settle disputes in advance of trial, the rules are unlikely to alter the incentive of clients to minimize litigation costs. Under the British Rule, higher legal fees (or transactions costs) will not improve a party's net recovery (since the fees at any level will be remitted to counsel), but increase risks of loss.

substantial fees… All the [lawyers] remain obliged to do is to explain their sudden eagerness to settle to clients who crave outright victory in court, who are now overly optimistic about the prospects of such victory, and eager for the trial to begin.[33]

In fairness, lawyers' incentives are far more complex in litigation than those resulting from hourly fees alone. To compete effectively for clients, a lawyer may need to demonstrate his or ability to manage and resolve cases efficiently. Further, a lawyer may encourage repeat business by efficiently resolving his or her cases. (This last point, however, suggests that larger businesses having greater risk of multiple lawsuits are likely to obtain more efficient service than businesses or individual clients involved in a one-time case.) Lastly, and perhaps contrary to economic theory, many lawyers take seriously their ethical obligation to put their clients' interests ahead of their own.

Zealous Representation of Clients, Prisoner's Dilemma, and Incentives to Make Discovery Costly and Inefficient

Entirely apart from possible economic incentives of lawyers to prolong litigation, the obligation of lawyers to zealously pursue their clients' interests creates strategic incentives to do the same. The strategic imperative to make litigation more, rather than less, contentious and costly stems not from combative personalities of litigators but from their rational acts to protect clients from being unfairly disadvantaged. Although cooperation between opposing parties in litigation would reduce costs for both sides, uncertainty about each other's good faith is likely to prevent them from achieving a mutually beneficial posture.

Although it seems irrational for parties to opt for litigation with more rather than less costs, the nature of litigation renders this choice both rational and likely. This result is evident from consideration of one of the seminal works in game theory—the "prisoner's dilemma." The prisoner's dilemma is a theoretical model that demonstrates how rational decision-making based on self-interest can—contrary to Adam Smith's invisible hand—precipitate worse results than seemingly irrational choices when parties face uncertainty about their opponents' next steps.[34]

The paradigm for the model is an example in which two suspects in a robbery have been arrested and are being questioned in separate rooms by the police. Without a confession, neither suspect is likely to be convicted of the robbery (although both could be convicted of a lesser charge). To induce a

---

[33] (Mnookin & Ross, 1995, p. 21).
[34] The concept of the prisoner's dilemma was developed by Rand Corporation scientists Merrill Flood and Melvin Dresher and was formalized by a Princeton mathematician, Albert W. Tucker.

confession, the police offer each suspect (or prisoner) the same deal: if one prisoner agrees to testify against the other and the other remains silent, the betrayer will go free and the silent prisoner will serve ten years. If each betrays the other, then each will serve five years. Lastly, if both prisoners stay silent (*i.e.*, cooperate with each other), they will both serve six months in jail for a minor charge.

The model, therefore, can be shown in the following matrix:

	Prisoner B is silent	Prisoner B testifies against Prisoner A (i.e., B betrays A)
Prisoner A is silent	Both Prisoners serve 6 months in jail	Prisoner A serves 10 years Prisoner B goes free
Prisoner A testifies against Prisoner B (i.e., A betrays B)	Prisoner A goes free and Prisoner B serves 10 years	Both Prisoners serve 5 years

The "dilemma" facing each prisoner is that his own best strategy depends upon what the other prisoner will do, but neither knows this critical information. Further, if both A and B act in their own self-interests, they end up worse than if neither does so.

In other words, if A acts only in his self-interest, he is likely to choose to betray Prisoner B, because this decision affords A the best outcome if B is either silent or betrays A. (Conversely, Prisoner B is likely to betray Prisoner A based on like reasoning.) However, as is evident from the matrix, blind pursuit of self-interest results in a worse outcome for both prisoners than cooperating with each other through silence.

The application of the prisoner's dilemma to litigation is clear. If neither party knows whether the other side will cooperate *(i.e.*, be forthcoming with information to facilitate a settlement), the best litigation strategy is to withhold information even though a mutually beneficial settlement could be reached if both parties disclosed their knowledge.

Indeed, litigation often compels inefficient outcomes of the prisoner's dilemma because it is not designed to determine the truth. Instead, it is a battle for control of the information needed to script the parties' self-interested portrayal of events for trial. Typically, at the outset of litigation, each party will control significant amounts of information both favorable and unfavorable to its position in the lawsuit. While each side will obviously want to shield its unfavorable information from its adversary, it may also want to shield favorable information in the hopes of delivering a surprise at trial. Conversely, each side will also want to acquire all of the other side's relevant information to prepare its own script and counter its opponent's story.

In litigation, the parties are expected, and obligated, to exchange information that will allow them each to prepare for trial and avoid being surprised. Discovery is conducted through requests for documents, interrogatories (*i.e.*, written questions), and depositions—all of which are expensive and time consuming.

Moreover, in federal court (and in most state courts), the range of permitted inquiry is extraordinarily broad. The Federal Rules of Civil Procedure provide:

> Unless otherwise limited by court order, the scope of discovery is as follows: Parties may obtain discovery regarding any nonprivileged matter that is relevant to any party's claim or defense—including the existence, description, nature, custody, condition, and location of any documents or other tangible things and the identity and location of persons who know of any discoverable matter. For good cause, the court may order discovery of any matter relevant to the subject matter involved in the action. ***Relevant information need not be admissible at the trial if the discovery appears reasonably calculated to lead to the discovery of admissible evidence.***[35]

In other words, the parties are allowed to discover not only evidence that they can use at trial, but information that may tell them where they might find admissible evidence. The breadth of permitted discovery, therefore, allows for "fishing expeditions" in which the parties cast wide nets in the hopes of finding something that they can use at trial. Although in many instances the courts will limit the scope of inquiry—for example, to a single division with a company or to specific individuals—some fishing is inevitable in complex cases.

While the costs of collecting, reviewing, copying, and proving information in response to even reasonable discovery requests can be substantial, such costs are, of course, increased—in some cases by multiples—by the adversarial process. Although witnesses are sworn "to tell the truth, the whole truth, and nothing but the truth," lawyers conducting discovery are not. As a general rule, neither side gives up any information to the other, unless it is specifically (and unambiguously) requested. This leads, of course, to remarkable creativity in the uncovering of ambiguities in an opponent's question. President Clinton's infamous response in his deposition about his relationship with Monica Lewinsky—explaining that "it depends on what the meaning of the word 'is' is"—hardly stands alone in the annals of careful responses to discovery.

---

[35] Fed.R.Civ.P. 26(b)(1).

For example, in one case, a great deal of time was spent preparing a witness for his upcoming deposition. After several "practice" depositions, the witness responded to questions from the opposing side during his real deposition like a pro. In trying to elicit answers about the resources that the witness used to prepare a report, the opposing lawyer asked, "How did you go about preparing your report?" The witness's accurate, but utterly useless response, was "with a pencil and paper."

In view of such gamesmanship, extracting useful information during discovery is often compared to "pulling teeth." Because neither side is likely to have a clear picture of the nature and scope of an opponent's information at the outset of a case and may not even know the identity of the most knowledgeable witness, discovery commonly requires multiple costly iterations. As each side learns about each other's likely argument and the range of information that may not yet have been disclosed, it repeats its discovery request and questions with greater specificity in hopes of obtaining more useful responses.

Litigants have a wide range of options for evading (and increasing the cost of) meaningful discovery. In some instances, a discovery request will be construed as broadly as possible to enable the party to complain to the court about the burden and cost of attempting to respond. In other instances, a request will be construed as narrowly as possible to limit the range of material information that will be provided in response. To the extent a request for discovery touches on privileged information that is immune from discovery, objections will be raised to shield information as broadly as possible. Of course, in some cases, a party will simply refuse to disclose relevant information and will require a court order to force it to do so.

Despite such tactics, in most cases, the parties eventually get most of the relevant information, and certainly enough to prepare for trial. A couple of factors eventually lead the parties to an equilibrium, where comparable levels of useful information are, or have been, exchanged. First, obstructionism cannot be so pronounced as to invite sanctions from the court. Second, the parties generally recognize that their own refusals to cooperate in discovery or obstructionism will be met in kind. As a result, each side will temper its obstructionism to avoid its debilitation—in other words, a form of the "mutually assured destruction" philosophy that informed cold-war diplomacy between the U.S. and the former Soviet Union. (In litigation, the point of equilibrium in discovery itself raises strategic issues for the parties, because a litigant that believes it controls more of the useful information at the outset of a case than its opponent will maneuver to establish equilibrium at a low level of disclosure, and the converse.)

In any event, and although every case raises unique discovery issues, it is abundantly clear that the less the parties and their counsels cooperate, the more expensive the case will be for both sides. Despite the certainty of this result, cooperation never dominates discovery. Even when the parties refrain from overt obstructionism in responding to discovery requests or overreach in making them, the rules of engagement between the parties imply that any cooperation will lie at the periphery of an intrinsically combative process.

Thus, however polite to his or her adversary, no party will ever volunteer to provide its opponent with the same information and assistance in understanding the information that it will provide its own litigation team. Instead, the adversaries must each elicit relevant information through the costly and iterative process previously described. An adversary will be considered "cooperative" in litigation if he or she merely agrees to respond, with some level of completeness and candor, to requests for discovery. Consequently, the difference between "cooperation" and obstructionism in litigation is simply a matter of the degree to which it exacerbates the inherently costly process of eliciting responses to unassisted (and sometime misdirected) inquiries.

Indeed, the ground rule for discovery is not to disclose "the truth, the whole truth, and nothing but the truth." Instead, discovery is governed by the strategic imperatives "to tell the truth when compelled to do so, to tell as little of the truth as necessary to avoid sanctions, and to tell more than the truth if a flood of information will be costly to the other side."

Because litigation does not, in fact, require bilateral strategic decisions without any information about an adversary's likely reaction, it can be argued that the inefficiencies of prisoner's dilemma can be avoided. Discovery and other pretrial procedures tend to be iterative. The parties, therefore, are able to consider and then respond to each other's acts of cooperation or contentiousness. However, Professors Ronald Gilson and Robert Mnookin explain that the iterations in litigation (which they term a "multiround prisoner's dilemma game") are unlikely as a theoretical matter to correct the problem, because each party will be concerned about his or her opponent's last move (which will not allow for a response).[36] In other words, each party will be worried about a non-cooperative action at the end of the case that might foreclose any subsequent response or retaliation.

Further, iterative negotiations between the parties over cooperation in discovery (with each party having the opportunity to respond to the other's actions), may not lead to cost-saving cooperation in any event. For example, the best known strategy for dealing with iterative rounds of prisoner's dilemma—

---

[36] (Gilson, 2000).

where each player knows whether or not its opponent cooperated in a prior round—is called "tit-for-tat." Tit-for-tat originated at a computer tournament organized by Robert Axelrod in 1980[37] in which he invited participants to develop strategies for "iterative prisoner's dilemma," where the players continue to interact with knowledge of prior rounds. Anatol Rapaport won with the simplest program entered in the tournament. The strategy was to cooperate in the first round of the game and then do whatever the opponent did in the previous round—either cooperate or act contrary to the opponent's interests (*i.e.*, defect).

After analyzing tit-for-tat and other strategies that performed well in the tournament, Axelrod identified four characteristics of a successful strategy. First, and most importantly, the strategy must be "nice" and not defect before the opponent does. Second, the strategy must be retaliatory—it must punish defection with defection. In the absence of retaliation, the cooperative player will lose badly. Third, the strategy must be "forgiving" and return to cooperation if the opponent does so. And finally, the strategy must be "nonenvious" and must be concerned not with winning more overall points than the opponent but with achieving the best result for itself (which may or may not involve winning). This means that tit-for-tat does not win every game against every type of strategy; instead, it is the best overall strategy for facing multiple or successive rounds of a game or negotiation. This last characteristic of tit-for-tat obviously raises problems in litigation, because winning is what ultimately matters.[38] On the other hand, it has been observed:

> [T]he general principal of cooperating with another agent prior to knowing how that agent will respond, and then reciprocating either cooperation or defection, appears from casual observation to one many people adopt to their advantage.... Be friendly, cooperative, and nice when initiating an interaction or negotiation, but don't hesitate to counterpunch if the other party punches first; moreover, having a reputation for adopting this policy may obviate the need to counterpunch (and hence the pain of initially being punched). Tit for tat works.[39]

---

[37] (Axelrod, 1984).

[38] On the other hand, "tit-for-tat" suggests another area of potential conflict between attorneys and their clients. In a given case, the client will care only about winning; his attorney, however, will be concerned about effectiveness for an entire career.

[39] (Dawes & Orbell, 2000), p. 63.

Although an appealing and, indeed, common strategy for discovery—cooperate until the other side does not—tit-for-tat is unlikely to constrain discovery costs through cooperation for several reasons. First, tit-for-tat only works if the parties can tell whether in fact their adversary is cooperating or merely feigning cooperation. In litigation, determining whether an adversary's cooperation is genuine may be difficult or even impossible without additional information. Given that adversaries in litigation do not trust each other and, indeed, in the zealous representation of clients, legal counsel are trained, if not obligated, to assume that their opponents are less than forthright, when an adversary's actions are in doubt, the safe assumption is that she is not telling the whole truth. Just because an adversary says she has produced all relevant records in discovery does not mean that she has done so.

In fact, the litigants have strong incentives to disguise obstruction as cooperation. Although overt obstructionism may lead to sanctions by the court, feigned and/or only partial cooperation may reduce this risk and offer some prospect for inducing misguided cooperation from the opposing side. Indeed, a common litigation tactic is to cooperate only as much as is necessary to avoid judicial sanctions. This, especially in complex cases, can leave significant room for faux cooperation. Further, because both parties are likely to be aware of this tactic, even good faith cooperation is likely to be discredited and lead to either feigned cooperation or none at all.

Passive Decision Makers

Another aspect of litigation that drives up its cost is its reliance on passive (and often unqualified or inexperienced) decision makers. Because the judge or jury often have no background related to the subject of the dispute, and because they are expected to passively observe the evidence and argument at trial, litigants must guess as to how much background or technical information is necessary. Almost invariably, litigating attorneys provide too much rather than too little background information to "educate" the decision maker(s). Indeed, to do otherwise could risk a malpractice claim based on lack of thoroughness.

One of the main methods in litigation for educating passive adjudicators with diverse qualifications is for each side to (redundantly) employ and present one or more expert witnesses. Even a cursory review of modern litigation, however, shows that modern "expert witnesses" are far more likely to testify as advocates (under the guise of expertise) than impartial educators of the court. Faced with this reality, each side hires experts to "cancel out" those of the other side. Again, the competing expert presentations may not precipitate the truth for the decision maker, who may be left to decide which experts look or speak better (rather than which has offered more accurate testimony).

Of course, all of the costly redundancy and excess preparation in litigation can be justified if it assures fair results in which recoveries and liabilities are allocated to the parties based upon informed decision-making by an impartial and well-qualified adjudicator. The theory of the adversary process is that, from the presentations of competing interpretations of fact and law, the truth will become evident to the impartial adjudicator or jury, who will then issue a just ruling in accordance with law.

Doubts about the ability of passive decision makers to impart high-quality justice are hardly new. In 1906, Dean Roscoe Pound of Harvard Law forcefully described the fallacy of the "sporting theory" of justice in a speech to the American Bar Association:

> [N]o less potent source of irritation lies in our American exaggerations of the common law contentious procedure. The sporting theory of justice, the "instinct of giving the game fair play," as Professor Wigmore has put it, is so rooted in the profession in America that most of us take it for a fundamental legal tenet. But it is probably only a survival of the days when a lawsuit was a fight between two clans in which change of venue had been taken to the forum. ...[I]n America we take it as a matter of course that a judge should be a mere umpire, to pass upon objections and hold counsel to the rules of the game, and that the parties should fight out their own game in their own way without judicial interference. We resent such interference as unfair, even when in the interests of justice. The idea that procedure must of necessity be wholly contentious disfigures our judicial administration at every point... The inquiry is not, What do substantive law and justice require? Instead, the inquiry is: Have the rules of the game been carried out strictly? If any material infraction is discovered, just as the football rules put back the offending team five or ten or fifteen yards, as the case may be, our sporting theory of justice awards new trials, or reverses judgments, or sustains demurrers in the interest of regular play.[40]

Pound's criticism of the adversary process focused on its exaltation of procedure above substance. In complex business disputes, the problem is more severe because a passive observation of competing presentations is especially unsuited to the task of ascertaining the truth, where such determinations may require a thorough understanding of the relevant industry, technology, law, and/

---

[40] (Pound, 1906).

or market. Unfortunately, it is unrealistic to expect that modern judges, however well intentioned and qualified, can devote the time needed to understand the context and complexities affecting commercial disputes in diverse fields when faced with dockets of hundreds or even thousands of pending cases. When juries are involved, the problem is magnified.[41]

Uncertainty as an Impediment to Settlement

One additional deficiency of litigation merits attention. Litigation not only requires extraordinary expenditures for uncertain results, it also impedes rather than promotes attempts by the parties to minimize the cost of their disputes through efficient settlement negotiations. Simply put, parties to a dispute are unlikely to reach a settlement as long as the rules governing their dispute are uncertain. These "rules" include not only what law applies and how it is interpreted, but also a determination of what facts are relevant to the allocation of liability.

The importance of clear rules for allocating liability is demonstrated, in part, by the "Coase Theorem," articulated by Professor Ronald Coase of the University of Chicago.[42] The Coase Theorem explains that, in the absence of transaction costs, an efficient outcome will be negotiated by adverse parties regardless of the initial allocation of property rights between them.

For example, if there are two adjacent farms, one with cows and one with corn, the two farmers have economic incentives to negotiate an economically optimal solution to the problem of keeping the cows from the corn—as long as a clear rule allocates responsibility for protecting the corn (and regardless of which farmer bears that responsibility). If the cow owner is obligated to protect the corn, but building a fence to protect the corn would cost him five times more than it would cost the corn owner to grow a type of corn that cows do not eat, he would have incentive to pay the corn owner to grow the alternative corn. Conversely, if the rule required the corn owner to protect his own corn (under

---

[41] Proponents of the jury system may legitimately argue that group decision making is often superior to decision making by an individual. See, *e.g.,* (Jonakait, 2006, pp. 41–63); (Vidmar & Hans, 2007, pp. 147–168). On the other hand, although studies suggest that judges often agree with jury verdicts, studies that take a close look at jury decision processes, such as case studies and mock jury studies, indicate that juries have difficulties with complex evidence and may not comprehend and follow legal instructions. (Vidmar & Hans, 2007, p. 168). In addition, "there can be little doubt that expert evidence, especially in cases with complex statistical evidence, poses difficulties for jurors. From what we can tell, jurors tend to give too little weight rather than too much weight to evidence they don't understand." (Vidmar & Hans, 2007, p. 189).

[42] (Coase, 1960).

the same economic facts), that farmer would also opt to change his corn rather than build an unnecessary fence.

Unstated in the Coase Theorem is the assumption that opposing parties will know both the facts and the rules affecting their interests. Although a host of "transaction cost" in the real world may prevent the "efficient outcome" or resolution of a dispute, no impediment is perhaps greater than disagreement as to the facts and uncertainty as to the rules. Thus, in our example, it is doubtful that the neighboring farmers could ever negotiate the optimal (or even a sensible) resolution if the rule governing their problem was in doubt and if they did not know that the cows were eating the corn, that a fence could be built, or that the farmer could grow distasteful corn.

Consistent with the Coase Theorem, economists have long assumed that the better litigants are able to estimate the outcome of a case, the more likely they are to reach a settlement.[43] In simplest form, if litigants know that the court will award the plaintiff $50,000, then it would be irrational for them to proceed with a costly trial, rather than settle for the amount of the certain outcome and thereby avoid the unnecessary costs. The corollary to this theory is anything that improves the litigants estimates of likely outcomes—such as discovery, experienced legal counsel, and prompt legal rulings by Court—will encourage settlements.[44]

The shortcoming of such theory, however, is that it may not consider the cost of mechanisms for improving the parties' estimates of likely outcomes. In litigation, key considerations—such as legal rulings that will govern the parties' claims, defenses, and evidence—are often unavailable until shortly before trial or even after a trial has begun. By contrast, an efficient dispute resolution system would more quickly provide the parties with such key information and at lower cost.

Conclusion

The inefficiency, redundancy, and questionable quality of litigation as a business decision-making process would not be tolerated in any other field. In litigation, much of the cost is justified as necessary to the workings of the adversary system. Rarely is the efficacy of the common law adversarial system questioned. In practice, however, little correlation seems to exist between the size of the investment in a case and the likelihood of a well-reasoned decision by an informed, committed, and qualified adjudicator.

---

[43] (Priest & Klein, 1984).
[44] (Ulen, 2006).

Alternatives to litigation commonly included within the rubric of "Alternative Dispute Resolution" (or "ADR") are more likely to address complex disputes efficiently. ADR processes can be tailored to the nature of the dispute and parties, and allow businesses engaged in good faith disputes to deploy their resources efficiently and with greater prospects for either a negotiated resolution or a high-quality decision.

CHAPTER IV: An Overview of Dispute Resolution Alternatives

Alternative Dispute Resolution ("ADR") refers to a procedures designed to manage and quickly resolve disagreements at lower cost than litigation while preserving the parties' business and other relationships. ADR procedures may include negotiations between disputants prior to litigation, negotiations during litigation mediation, early neutral evaluation, neutral fact finding, binding or nonbinding arbitration, mock mini-trials, and private judging. Each method has pros and cons that must be evaluated in light of the nature of the dispute and the parties.

Without a doubt, the most common forms of ADR for business disputes are negotiation, mediation, and arbitration. With respect to international business disputes, arbitration may be more commonplace than court proceedings because it enables parties from different countries with different legal systems to resolves disputes on a level playing field, with neither party having a potentially substantial "home court" advantage.

As background for the remainder of this book, this chapter provides a general overview of the principal forms of ADR deployed in commercial disputes—negotiation, mediation, and arbitration.

Negotiation Before Litigation

Perhaps the simplest and most common form of ADR is for the disputing parties to negotiate a resolution. In recent years, it has been common in business contracts for the parties to formally require each other to attempt to resolve disputes in negotiation before resorting to litigation or arbitration. In particular, the parties may require sequential escalation of disputes from line managers to department heads and/or to CEOs before seeking intervention.

The success of mandatory negotiation schemes is difficult to evaluate. Although required negotiation schemes may seem a sensible and low-cost predicate to formal dispute mechanisms, they carry a few risks that merit consideration.

First, by setting aside a required period for negotiations, such as 15 or 30 days, a party may be compelled to suffer increased harm before seeking intervention.   During the negotiation period, for example, a party may be prevented from terminating a costly service or consulting contract on one hand, or accepting a project for a different customer on the other.

Second, while a company's senior managers may have a broader perspective on the potential benefits or risks of pursuing a dispute and/or on the relationship between the parties, they may not have a detailed understanding of the facts giving rise to conflicts.   Consequently, the escalated negotiations may be ineffective and serve merely to give each side time to prepare for legal battles. (Indeed, in one of my cases, the parties to such an agreement filed competing lawsuits against each other in different jurisdictions within hours of expiration of the "negotiation" period.)

Negotiation during Litigation

Although much of this book focuses on avoiding litigation entirely, effective negotiation during litigation can itself significantly reduce costs.   Although settlement on the eve of trial saves far less than an early or pre-litigation settlement, it nonetheless avoids significant costs.   The cost of a trial can equal or exceed the cost of many months of discovery and motions..   And a trial is hardly the end of expense: post-trial briefs and appeals can add years and sizeable sums to the cost of a case.

Negotiation during litigation raises its own set of challenges.   Opposing litigation counsel may be too busy preparing for trial, and have developed too much distrust, to negotiate effectively.   In addition, litigation counsel may be concerned about exhibiting weakness or making harmful disclosures of evidence or strategy during negotiation.

For such reasons, it is sometime beneficial to assign or retain separate "settlement counsel" to negotiate settlement terms while litigation counsel marches inexorably to trial.   In one of my cases litigated in the "rocket docket" of the federal court in Northern Virginia—where cases are commonly scheduled for completion within 6 months—the pace of trial preparation simply did not allow for the distraction of negotiations that might prove fruitless.   A colleague in my firm, who had not been involved in the case, agreed to take responsibility for settlement negotiations, and he successfully orchestrated a settlement on the eve of trial.

Apart from trial preparation demands that may prevent litigation counsel from taking the lead in settlement talks, in some instances trial counsel may simply not be well suited for the task.   Zealous trial advocates may have different skills than those best suited for settlement talks or may be impeded in settlement talks by "a seemingly irreconcilable set of contradictory models for behavior."[45] Because of the potential for increased legal fees, however, clients may be reluctant to adopt a dual-track approach in litigation. On the other hand, the cost of settlement counsel may be modest in relation to cost of the litigation, and the potential for a faster and better settlement may far outweigh the additional expense.[46]

Mediation

Mediation is "a process in which a neutral person or persons facilitate communications between the disputants to assist them in reaching a mutually acceptable agreement."[47] Because a mediator has no decision-making authority, he cannot render a binding decision on the parties. A mediator does not hear testimony or evidence, and has no authority to impose a decision on the parties. Nonetheless, even when mediation does not result in a complete settlement, it may enable the parties to narrow the scope of their dispute or decide upon expedited procedures for resolving remaining areas of conflict.

Mediation typically proceeds in three main stages. If the mediation does not result in a complete settlement, the parties may extend the process based upon progress made during the initial session.

First, the parties (and their counsel) and the mediator convene in a joint session. After opening remarks by the mediator, the parties are afforded the opportunity to state their respective positions and objective for resolving the dispute.

Second, the parties separate and the mediator engages in shuttle diplomacy. The mediator explores the dispute with the parties in confidence and seeks common ground that may provide a basis for resolution. The mediator will relay proposals and responses between the parties after helping them to frame their dialog in a constructive manner. The mediator may also serve as an impartial sounding board and provide each side with a "reality check."

Third, the parties and mediator will reconvene in a joint session to iron out final details of an agreement. If a full settlement has not been reached, the parties may nonetheless agree to remove certain of the issue from the case, to an efficient procedure for resolving remaining issues (in lieu of litigation), to exchange a limited range of information and thereafter to reconvene, and so on. In many cases, mediation initiates a continuing dialog and process for achieving a settlement in a cost effective manner.

---

[45] (Yarn, 2000, p. 77).

[46] (Craver, 2005, p. 369)("While clients might initially fear this dual-track approach would increase legal fees, the efficient operation of this system should have the opposite effect. Cases would be settled more often and more expeditiously.")

[47] California Evidence Code § 111.5.

The Mediation Process

Joint Session

- Mediator's Opening Remarks
- Parties' Positions and Goals

Private Sessions and Shuttle Diplomacy

- Confidential Discussions
- Mediator Frames Dialog and Relays Proposals

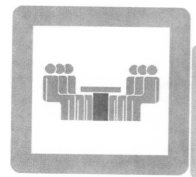

Reconvene Joint Session

- Final Agreement, or
- Recap Progress
- Establish Framework for Settlement

Like other forms of ADR, a hallmark of mediation is confidentiality. Statements made during mediation are not typically admissible in litigation, and the parties (and mediator) can further assure confidentiality by agreement. As discussed more fully in Chapter V, because a skilled mediator can filter confidential information and frame the parties' discussion in ways that enhance the likelihood of success, mediation can enable parties to reach mutually beneficial agreement in circumstances in which direct negotiations would fail.

In most cases, the benefits of mediation far outweigh its risks. The principal risks related to failed mediation are: (i) its comparatively modest cost and time commitment; and (ii) its potential for educating an opponent about a party's strengths, weaknesses, and strategies. In most business litigation, the cost of mediation is immaterial to the cost of the overall dispute. The risk of disclosure can be addressed by clearly instructing the mediator as to information that can, and cannot, be shared with the opposing party.

The benefits of mediation are, by contrast, potentially substantial. Over 90 percent of litigated cases settle prior to judgment. Indeed, in 2004, the Litigation Section of the American Bar Association undertook a "major project" termed the "Vanishing Trial" project to better understand the causes of (and to commiserate) the decline in trial rates over the past 50 years. The ABA's analysis demonstrates how rarely, in fact, the filing of complaint leads to trial:

> In federal courts, the decline in trials has been steep and dramatic. In 1962, there were 5,802 civil trials in the federal courts and 5,097 criminal trials, for a total of 10,899. In 1985, total federal trials had risen to 12,529. By 2002, however, trials had dropped to 4,569 civil trials and 3,574 criminal trials. *Thus, our federal courts actually tried fewer cases in 2002 than they did in 1962, despite a five-fold increase in the number of civil filings and more than a doubling of the criminal filings over the same time frame. In 1962, 11.5 percent of federal civil cases were disposed of by trial. By 2002, that figure had plummeted to 1.8 percent.*[48]

To the extent that mediation expedites the settlement process, it can generate substantial cost savings. Further, and unlike court rulings and arbitration, mediation may enable the parties to renew or develop mutually beneficial business arrangements based on areas of common interest identified in the mediation process.

---

[48] (Refo, 2004). Although less accurate data were developed with respect to state courts, the data studied from 22 states indicated a 28 percent decline from 1976 and that 99.4 percent of filed cases were resolved in advance of trial.

Arbitration

Arbitration refers to the hearing and adjudication of a dispute by an impartial third party or parties (referred to as "neutrals" or "arbitrators") selected and authorized by the parties to resolve their dispute. An arbitrator's authority to decide a dispute depends entirely on the agreement of the parties. Thus, in selecting arbitration as a means for resolving disputes, the parties not only select the arbitrator (or agree upon a method for choosing an arbitrator), they also determine the scope of the disputes that the arbitrator will be authorized to decide upon and the rules or procedures to be followed by the arbitrator in deciding a matter.

As a practical matter, the parties seldom spell out the rules to be followed by the arbitrator, but instead rely upon rules developed over the years by either dispute resolution organizations, such as the American Arbitration Association, the Center for Dispute Resolution, the International Chamber of Commerce, etc., or model rules for such disputes, such as UNCITRAL. Further, businesses often decide upon an organization to administer the arbitration, *i.e.*, to assist with the selection and management of the arbitrator and dispute process, rather than to submit a matter for ad hoc arbitration by an individual arbitrator operating independently.

The basic elements of arbitration are: (1) a third-party decision maker chosen by the parties; (2) a mechanism to ensure neutrality in the decision; (3) an opportunity for the parties to be heard; and (4) a binding decision.[49] In most arbitration cases, an agreement to arbitrate is included in a clause in the contract governing the parties. Generally, mandatory arbitration clauses are enforceable.[50]

Historically, arbitration has been considered faster and less expensive than litigation. Further, by permitting the parties to select the arbitrator, arbitration can provide some assurance that the decision maker will have knowledge and experience related to the subject matter of the dispute and can avoid the risk of an unfavorable or unsuitable judicial assignment and jury.

Dispute Management and Avoidance

As in medicine, prevention is generally far more cost effective than efforts to remedy problems after they arise. Even when disputes cannot be prevented, effective management can prevent small disputes from growing into large ones.

---

[49] *Cheng-Canindin v. Renaissance Hotel Assoc.*, 50 Cal.App. 4th 676, 57 Cal.Rptr.2d 867, 872 (1996).

[50] *See, e.g., Madden v. Kaiser Foundation Hospitals*, 17 Cal. 3d 699, 131 Cal.Rptr. 886 (1976).

The Arbitration Process

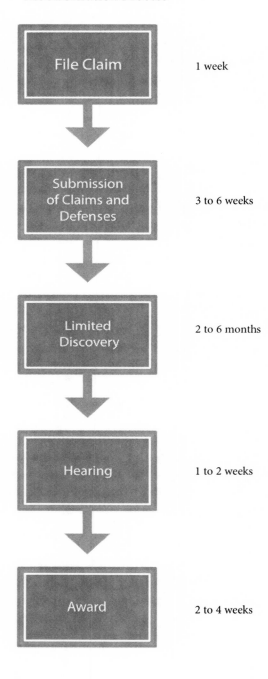

The key to dispute management is simply to recognize, plan for, and respond to common areas of conflict in commercial agreements. Although the nature of predictable disputes varies across industries, many industries exhibit a pattern of predictable conflicts that can be managed and contained.

For example, in both information technology ("IT") and construction projects, disputes over the scope of work that the vendor or contractor must complete without additional compensation are commonplace, as are disputes over cost increases arising from project delays. Most IT and construction agreements require the customer to submit written requests to modify the project. The vendor must then, within a specified period, identify any likely cost and timing effects of the request. However, many such contracts fail to establish a protocol for addressing disagreements as to whether a customer's instructions are an increase in the scope of the project (as the vendor may contend) or simply instructions related to implementation of the project's scope. IT and construction contracts also frequently fail to set rules for the parties in the event of delays (and the parties' inevitable conflicting arguments as to which party was responsible).

Contract provisions that attempt to specify procedures for changing project scope or addressing other likely areas of conflict are more important for establishing expectations and for dispute management than for their legal significance. Obviously, even in the absence of a contract term describing procedures for "change," the parties could modify contract terms by amendment. The value of a protocol should not, however, be understated. One of the principal reasons IT projects fail is the inability of project personnel to document and agree upon changes in project responsibilities or scope. Absent consistent and complete documentation—including terms and conditions of project modification—evaluating the project's success or failure (at least for the purpose of assigning responsibility) can be difficult and sometimes impossible.

CHAPTER V: Why Mediation Can Often Resolve Disputes More Effectively than Direct Negotiation

As the cost of business litigation continues to soar, the corresponding incentives to seek less costly means of resolving disputes should encourage increased reliance on arbitration, mediation, and other modes of ADR.

As an alternative to litigation, mediation is perhaps the most common means used to resolve disputes. Because it allows the parties to decide and control their own fates, it provides a relatively painless introduction to ADR. Even when meditation does not resolve all disputed issues, it can narrow the scope and expense of litigation and/or initiate a dialogue that ultimately allows for resolution.

Perhaps the greatest barrier to greater reliance on mediation is a general lack of understanding as to how and why it works. When a litigation team includes qualified legal counsel and sophisticated business people with substantial experience negotiating deals, the expense of a third-party mediator may not seem justified. The parties may believe that if a deal or settlement is to be reached, mediation is no more likely to succeed than one-on-one negotiation between the sophisticated parties and/or their counsel. Such a belief, however, is wrong.

Mediation can, and often does, succeed in resolving disputes, because it not only affords the opportunity to craft agreements that address non-economic interests (*e.g.*, an apology or other form of recognition) or create value for both parties (*e.g.*, incorporating a business deal into a settlement), but also—and more importantly—because a skilled mediator can address and overcome a variety of obstacles to a settlement that are inherent in direct negotiations between the parties.

Moreover, sometimes mediation is needed to reach a settlement simply because a skilled mediator may be able to overcome one or both parties' poor negotiation skills.

While some of the obstacles to successful direct negotiations are obvious (*e.g.*, animosity and lack of trust), others are not. After discussing economic and non-monetary bases for settlement and some of the impediments to successful direct negotiations, this chapter discusses how a skilled mediator can achieve fair settlements that the parties are unlikely to achieve on their own (or, at least, unlikely to achieve until after most of the cost of litigation has been incurred).

An Economic Model for Settlement of Commercial Disputes

Although personal conflicts may center on intangible human needs and interests, business disputes most commonly focus on money and related economic matters. The economic focus of business disputes does not result from any lack of personal interest or emotion of the participants. In other words, it is not because—as in populist ideals—businesses are faceless entities concerned only with cold hard cash, but because personal and business disputes differ in some key respects.

In many (if not most) business disputes, the person or persons empowered to reach a settlement are different from those involved in the conflict itself. For example, a business may buy defective equipment because a sales agent allegedly misleads a purchasing manager. If the matter escalates to litigation, however, neither the sales agent nor the purchasing manager is likely to be authorized to settle the dispute. Instead, senior executives may make settlement decisions, with the possible participation of the defendants' insurers. As a result, noneconomic facts (*e.g.*, a desire for an apology) are likely less important to the resolution.

Similarly, organizations involved in a dispute will comprise numerous individuals with diverse outlooks and agendas. These individuals, however, commonly share an interest in the economic well being of their organization. As a result, each party's internal dynamics may lead to a focus on economic, rather than other, factors that could affect a settlement.

Settlement of a purely economic dispute should, therefore, depend upon the parties' respective appraisals of the value of the case, as follows:

Plaintiff's Value = *Probability of success x expected recovery*[51] *- litigation cost – opportunity costs*

Defendant's Value = *Probability of loss x expected payout + litigation cost + opportunity costs*

Settlement Condition: *Plaintiff's Value ≤ Defendant's Value*

The "Settlement Condition" refers to the fact that a case should settle whenever the defendant expects the case to cost more than the plaintiff expects to recover.

---

[51] A more refined statistical appraisal of settlement value is to consider the sum of probable outcomes. In other words, a plaintiff may assess the likely outcome as: 20% probability of no recovery + 40% probability of $100,000 recovery + 30% probability of $300,000 + 10% probability of $1 million, in which case his or her assessment equals $0 + $40,000 + 90,000 + 100,000, or $230,000.

Negotiation experts describe such circumstances as creating a "zone of possible agreement" or "ZOPA."[52]

In many commercial negotiations, the role of each side's negotiator is to obtain as much value from the deal as possible. If a seller is willing to sell widgets for $60 and the buyer is willing to buy them for $100, then the deal will create a surplus (or ZOPA) of $40. The skill of each side's negotiator will determine which side garners most of that $40 surplus. (Of course, expert negotiators may be able to modify the basic deal to increase the surplus available to benefit both sides by, for example, including additional products or services in the deal.)

In litigation, however, often the key issue is whether the Settlement Condition is met (or a ZOPA even exists). Because of biased perceptions, both parties are likely to value the potential recovery or cost of a case unrealistically. Worse, the parties' strategic incentive to withhold information may prevent them from identifying settlement opportunities.

Fortunately, and as discussed below, a skilled mediator can often overcome such impediments to efficient settlement of business disputes. A mediator may be able to persuade the parties to adopt realistic case valuations and, through shuttle diplomacy, bridge the information gap between them. In addition, and equally important, a skilled mediator may be able to overcome internal conflicts or poor negotiation skills that may scuttle an efficient settlement.

Interest-Based Approaches to Health Care and Workplace Disputes

Although it is possible to consider any dispute, claim or defense in the context of an economic equation, to do so would misleadingly characterize the nature of most interpersonal disputes. In healthcare and employment matters, disputes often arise and escalate as the result of miscommunication, hurt feelings, and a host of other intangible considerations. Although economic factors, such as those discussed above, may be important elements of settlement discussions, they may not be the important or dispositive ones.

In healthcare, for example, patients' and their families' desire for open, caring communication by providers who have made mistakes cannot be underestimated. A 2006 Consensus Statement of the Harvard Hospitals explains:

> In one British survey, 92% of patients believed that a patient should always be told if a complication has occurred, and 81% of patients believed that a patient should not only be informed of a complication but also be given detailed information on possible adverse outcomes. In a British survey

---

[52] (Malhotra & Bazerman, 2007, p. 23-24).

of 227 patients and relatives who were taking legal action in malpractice cases, plaintiffs wanted greater honesty, an appreciation of the severity of the trauma they had suffered, and assurances that lessons had been learned from their experiences.

When they are injured by physicians' mistakes, patients may feel hurt, betrayed, devalued, humiliated, and afraid. By taking responsibility and apologizing, the physician acknowledges these feelings, shows an understanding of their impact, and begins to make amends. The apology helps to restore the patient's dignity and begin the healing process. It also helps the physician deal with his own emotional trauma. On the other hand, failing to admit error and express regret "adds insult to injury" by not fully respecting the patient's situation.[53]

Unfortunately, the prevailing legal wisdom for decades has been for healthcare providers to say nothing about medical errors because of concern that any statements could be used to prosecute a malpractice claim. Although plainly correct when viewed through the lens of pre-litigation posturing, such advice has a substantial risk of fostering litigation rather than discouraging it. As the Harvard Hospitals explain:

> Contrary to what many physicians believe, there is little evidence that apologizing increases the risk of a malpractice suit. In fact, experience in malpractice cases indicates just the opposite: that the failure to communicate openly, take responsibility, and apologize contributes to patients' anger. Some malpractice lawyers contend that two-thirds of malpractice suits stem from a failure to take responsibility, apologize, and communicate openly.[54]

Mediation offers both providers and patients the opportunity to candidly address such non-economic needs and interest without fear that their discussions will provide fodder for ensuing litigation.

Further, and the extent that financial interests become part of the provider-patient dialog, a caring, respectful, and responsive dialog about medical errors can dramatically affect the nature of monetary demands. For example, an affected patient may feel satisfied and fully compensated by a waiver of fees related to a hospital stay or course of treatment and/or a relatively small payment that evidences the providers' acceptance of responsibility and sense of fair play.

---

[53] (Harvard Hospitals, 2006)
[54] Ibid.

As in healthcare, mediation of workplace disputes can identify and address a broad range of intangible factors that may not only lead to disputes but seriously disrupt productivity and the work environment. In many respects, each workplace establishes its own society with its own rules and protocols. Because of the innumerable opportunities for miscommunication and conflicting interpretations of an organizations' social norms, mediation is ideally suited to address workplace disputes when they arise to prevent their expansion into costly disruptions and litigation.

Information Risks

The first obstacle to direct negotiations—strategic information risk—stems from the fact that each party's objective in litigation is not so much to reach a just resolution for all, but to win. Further, one of the key components of success in litigation is strategic control of information, as each side strives to disclose or obtain information supporting its position while suppressing harmful information. As discussed above, the information risks and rewards associated with litigation may replicate the prisoner's dilemma that discourages cooperation in litigation, even though to cooperate might significantly reduce wasteful litigation costs for both (or all) parties.

A skilled mediator can help resolve the dilemma for both parties and overcome this informational void. In common mediation practice, a mediator will advise each party that he or she will keep information strictly confidential when asked to do so. Assuming that he or she engenders sufficient trust from each side to obtain information that would otherwise have been unavailable in the negotiation, the mediator can then serve as a filter to identify possible areas of agreement that would not otherwise become apparent, while preserving each side's strategic position in the event the negotiation fails.

Reactive Devaluation

Reactive devaluation refers to the fact that the parties to a dispute are likely to assess offers or proposals differently depending on who makes them. In particular, each side to a dispute is likely to value a proposal made by the other side less than if the same proposal was made by their own side.

A simple example illustrates this point. In a dispute over $100,000 in unpaid fees, the plaintiff may believe that he or she has a 50% chance of success and, therefore, enters a settlement discussion hoping for a $50,000 settlement. If, however, the defendant immediately offers $50,000 to settle the case, more often than not the plaintiff will reject the offer. Why?

Two related factors contribute to this result. First, most parties assume that their opponent will not start negotiations with a best and final offer. Consequently, the plaintiff will reject the offer simply in hopes of getting a better deal as the negotiation (or litigation) progresses.

Second, the plaintiff's decision to reject the offer may reflect a recalibration of his or her assessment of the case, because of the information conveyed for (or at least attributed to) the settlement offer. In others words, at the start of the negotiation, the plaintiff assessed his or her probability of success at 50 percent based on his or her own information. In making this assessment, the plaintiff should know (or reasonably suspect) that the defendant has additional information that has not been disclosed. Consequently, the plaintiff will use information and/or clues conveyed in the negotiation to adjust his or her evaluation of the case. When the defendant offers $50,000, the plaintiff may reasonably conclude that the defendant has information harmful to the defense and/or beneficial to the plaintiff, *i.e.*, that the offer is a "sign of weakness."

This phenomenon can be readily seen in other contexts as well. One reason that auction sales often generate high prices for sellers is that bidders gain confidence in the value of a piece based on other bidders' interest in the same item. For this reason, auction houses often start the bidding at a price lower than the seller is willing to sell (*i.e.*, the reserve price) in an effort to generate excitement and interest in a piece.

A skilled mediator can overcome reactive devaluation, at least in part, by the manner in which he or she makes offers and counteroffers. When the opposing party posits an offer as the mediator's "idea" or as a difficult concession, the potential for devaluation of a good faith offer can be diminished.

Agency Problems and Intraparty Conflicts

Agency problems in negotiation refer to problems arising from the differing, and sometimes conflicting, interests of principals and their negotiating team (or clients and their counsel). Likewise, conflicting objectives within an organization or among co-parties can impair, or even preclude, efficient negotiations.

With respect to legal counsel, there has long been an intractable debate as to whether legal counsel helps or hinders settlement negotiations. The cynical view suggests that while a client may want to resolve a dispute as quickly and inexpensively as possible, its counsel, if paid hourly, may prefer a more protracted dispute. The problem with this argument is that it assumes that lawyers have serial relationships with clients who are either indifferent to legal costs or are unsophisticated. To the extent an attorney strives to develop a long-term relationship with a client and/or a reputation for efficiency, his or her financial incentives may more closely align with those of the client.

Perhaps the most difficult obstacle to settlement arises when multiple organizations, individuals, or parties must reach agreement in a situation in which their interests align for some purposes, but not for others. One common example of this problem is where a defendant's insurer has agreed to pay defense costs but has reserved the right to deny insurance coverage for liability. In such cases, a party may be reluctant to agree to a reasonable settlement because of concern that it would provide a basis for its insurer to deny coverage. Even more complex are cases in which a claim is covered by overlapping insurance policies and insurers, each of whom reserved rights and has incentives to foist the cost of settlement on either the party or the other insurer(s).

In such cases, a mediator needs, in effect, to resolve multiple disputes at once or, at times, persuade the parties to follow an efficient sequence and agree upon strategies and procedures for resolving residual matters.

For example, there are many cases in which conflicts among co-parties might block a settlement, even when it is abundantly clear that the cost of litigation would far exceed the amount in dispute. Indeed, as the number of parties in litigation increases, the cost increases, but the prospects for an efficient settlement diminish because of the diverse interests of co-parties and/or their insurers.

In a recent lawsuit, the plaintiff's building was damaged by a construction project involving multiple entities—the project sponsor, the contractor, the site engineer, and the project designer. Repairing the damage to the building was expected to cost less than $500,000. Although the combined litigation costs of the five parties would greatly exceed the cost of the repair, the case did not promptly settle because of finger-pointing among the defendants (and their insurers). As in the prisoner's dilemma, by pursing their own self-interests in denying liability, the defendants' costs arising from the damage far exceeded the amounts ultimately in dispute.

By contrast, mediation in a second matter was able to avoid significant unnecessary litigation costs by resolving simultaneously two interrelated disputes. The plaintiff alleged that the defendant violated a software license and infringed plaintiff's copyright by making unauthorized use of the software after expiration of the license. Defendant denied infringement and asserted that it had created its own alternative, noninfringing product. Meanwhile, defendant had insurance with two carriers who agreed to share the defense costs, but reserved the right to deny coverage.

As in the first case, litigation costs were likely to exceed the amount the plaintiff would recover if it proved its claims. Although plaintiff had some prospect for punitive damages under copyright law, a successful claim would most likely have resulted in the award of modest damages due to lost license revenues. Meanwhile, the primary dispute between the plaintiff and defendant had the potential to cost each side more than the likely recovery (because the case was unlikely be resolved on summary judgment and would involve multiple experts, etc.). Further, potential litigation between and among the defendant and its insurers over coverage risked additional costs in excess of the disputed amount.

After identifying the inevitably inefficient consequences of litigation, mediation facilitated settlement among the parties (and the insurers) that included both a renewed business arrangement between the plaintiff and defendant (which would not have been a possible outcome of litigation) and payments by the defendant and the insurers that were, on an individual basis, far less than the likely litigation costs that they respectively would have incurred had the litigation continued.

Overcoming Distrust

Finally, a skilled mediator can play a critical role in mitigating, and reducing unnecessary costs created by, the parties' distrust of each other. Obviously, one of the most significant obstacles to the efficient resolution of disputes is the fact that parties are unlikely to believe each other's versions (and/or interpretations) of the facts and relevant law. Although the problem of distrust is not systemically (or strategically) different in direct negotiations and mediation, mediation can help reduce the time and cost of overcoming distrust as an impediment to dispute resolution.

Indeed, the extraordinary cost of discovery in modern litigation stands as a testament to the costs created by unresolved distrust. Because the parties disbelieve each other, and pretrial discovery seeks not only information that each party intends to rely upon at trial, but also to invalidate each other's respective arguments and support. Thus, a discovery request for a party's relevant email messages includes not only a request for the messages themselves, but also for information about the party's respective information technology systems, document retention practices, email policies, etc., for the purpose of determining whether *all* of the relevant email messages have in fact been disclosed.

Assisting the parties to overcome (or at least accommodate) their mutual distrust is a potentially important and cost-saving element of mediation. Although neither party may believe the legal analysis of the opposing party, they both may accept an assessment provided by a qualified mediator. Further, short of resolving the dispute at an initial mediation session, a skilled mediator may help the parties identify key areas of discovery and disclosure necessary to achieve a settlement and thereby avoid protracted discovery and related disputes.

Reality Checking and Case Valuation

Returning to our premise that business disputes are typically resolved based on economic criteria, the overarching benefit of access to a skilled mediator is his or her ability to act as a credible sounding board and proponent for each side to adopt realistic assumptions in evaluating their relative appraisals of the Settlement Value. As explained in Chapter II, litigation invites skewed perspectives of prospects for success, litigations costs, and control.

Thus, a mediator may provide a reality check for each party's assessment of likely damages and prospects for success. If done well, the parties themselves will reappraise their assessments based on the mediator's input and questions, and the mediator need not interject his or her own appraisal of the case. For example, by providing a structure for both settlement discussions and analysis, a mediator may help the parties appreciate the implications of litigation risk, litigation costs, and opportunity costs to their expectations for the case. (In some instances, though, an objective evaluation by the mediator may be helpful or necessary.)

For example, neither party may fully appreciate the litigation and opportunity costs of pursuing their dispute. Opportunity costs refer to the beneficial uses of time, money, and other resources that are forgone because of their use in the chosen alternative. In commercial disputes, opportunity costs typically include profits that could have been earned with the time and money devoted to the litigation, but they also include lost opportunity to develop or reestablish mutually beneficial arrangements with the opposing party, where appropriate.

Likewise, the full extent of litigation costs may not be completely appreciated by the parties. Not only does litigation commonly cost more in fees and expenses than predicted, it may impose a host of related but indirect costs on the parties. For example, litigation may result in adverse publicity, reduced morale, and financial uncertainty, and it may impair routine internal communications and/or otherwise disrupt company operations.

By encouraging the parties to consider and attempt to quantify such costs, a mediator may move them closer to resolving their disputes. And by facilitating a rational evaluation of the prospects for a dispute, a mediator may help the parties reach agreement far sooner than if left to their own devices.

Indeed, a recent study suggests that a mediator's experience in dispute resolution and awareness of the biases affecting case evaluation can improve the parties' settlement decisions. The study of public settlement offers in California, referenced in Chapter II, demonstrates that decisions to proceed to trial rather than settle are often mistakes. The study notes, however, "attorneys trained and experienced in dispute resolution, and perhaps more cognizant of framing biases, may have a salutary effect on attorney/litigant decision making."[55] The study explains that "[a]n attorney-mediator's representation of a plaintiff is associated with a 21 percent reduction in plaintiff decision error, and the presence of an attorney-mediator representing any party is correlated with a dramatic reduction in the overall incidence of decision error."[56]

---

[55] (Kiser, Asher, & McShane, 2008, p. 589).
[56] Ibid.

CHAPTER VI: Arbitration: A Potentially Efficient Alternative

If parties to a dispute are unable to reach agreement on their own through either negotiation or mediation, they will likely submit the dispute to a third party—a judge or neutral party (in this case an arbitrator)—for a decision. The inefficiency of the U.S. court system as a means for resolving business disputes has been discussed in Chapter III. This Chapter discusses the promise and potential pitfalls of private arbitration—the most common adjudicative alternative.

As discussed below, although arbitration can be expected to produce higher-quality decisions than litigation, the cost efficiency of arbitration depends largely on how well the arbitrator manages the process.

Background

The notion that national courts operate too slowly and inefficiently for business is hardly new. In medieval times, separate merchant courts were often established at seasonal fairs to address commercial matters quickly and cost effectively in accordance with trade practice and custom, sometimes referred to as Merchant Law, or *lex merchant*. Although medieval merchants had the option of pursuing their claims in common law courts, the time-consuming legal process was likely incompatible with the development of trade.[57]

Although commentators sometimes considered the medieval commercial courts to operate independent of national courts and enforcement mechanisms under the theory that the law merchant was "voluntarily produced, voluntarily adjudicated, and voluntarily enforced," Sachs suggests that, in fact, enforcement was backed by the coercive power of local governing authorities.[58] The history of modern business arbitration suggests that coercive enforcement, such as through national courts, is a necessary element of any arbitration scheme.

Thus, business arbitration became a viable alternative to litigation upon the adoption of laws providing for judicial enforcement of arbitration awards. In the United States, the first such law was enacted in New York state in 1920,

---

[57] (Sachs, 2006) (Providing an overview of a medieval commercial court and discussing some misconceptions about the *lex merchant*).

[58] (Sachs, 2006, pp. 697–705).

which was followed by the enactment of the Federal Arbitration Act (FAA) in 1925.[59] Both the New York statute and the FAA allowed for development of business arbitration in the United States by providing for judicial enforcement of arbitration agreements and arbitral awards, and setting forth the limited grounds upon which such an award could be overturned or vacated.

Section 10 of the FAA, for example, authorizes the federal courts to overturn an arbitral award only:

1. Where the award was procured by corruption, fraud, or undue means.
2. Where there was evident partiality or corruption in the arbitrators, or either of them.
3. Where the arbitrators were guilty of misconduct in refusing to postpone the hearing, upon sufficient cause shown, or in refusing to hear evidence pertinent and material to the controversy; or of any other misbehavior by which the rights of any party have been prejudiced.
4. Where the arbitrators exceeded their powers, or so imperfectly executed them that a mutual, final, and definite award upon the subject matter submitted was not made.

Equally important, the FAA specifically provides for enforcement of arbitration agreements. In other words, after signing an arbitration agreement, a party cannot unilaterally decide to pursue claims covered by the agreement in court. Upon the complaint of the opposing party and proof of the agreement, the court "shall make an order directing the parties to proceed with arbitration in accordance with the terms of the agreement."

An Overview of Business Arbitration

In simplest terms, there are five basic steps in arbitration: (i) selection of the arbitrator(s) by the parties; (ii) submissions of claims, counterclaims, and defenses to the arbitrator(s); (iii) an arbitration hearing at which the parties present testimony and evidence; and (iv) the arbitration decision. Noticeably absent from the foregoing list is discovery. Although discovery is not necessary to implement an arbitration agreement, most commercial arbitration includes a prehearing exchange of documentary evidence between the parties and some degree of discovery. As discussed below, the scope and extent of discovery in commercial arbitration can vary significantly from case to case and, as in litigation, can dramatically affect the parties' costs.

---

[59] 9 U.S.C. §1 *et seq.*

The true nature of arbitration comes to light when compared with litigation. Importantly, both litigation and arbitration (in the U.S.) are adversarial processes in which each side submits its interpretation of fact and law to a passive adjudicator—judge, jury, or arbitrator—who is expected to decide the matter based upon the record presented by the parties. Still, as the chart below summarizes, there are important differences between arbitration and litigation that are worth considering.

Process Element or Procedure	Litigation	Arbitration
Pool of potential decision makers	Politically appointed or elected judges; jurors chosen from the public at large.	Unlimited
Selection of decision maker(s)	The court, in accordance with internal operating rules, selects the judge without party involvement. Jurors are randomly selected from the public and empanelled in accordance with court procedures, which typically allow parties to veto some potential jurors but not to select jurors.	By the parties or pursuant to a procedure agreed upon by the parties.
Forum and venue	Chosen by plaintiff in accordance with jurisdictional statutes.	As agreed by the parties.
Procedural rules	Federal or State Rules of Civil Procedure.	As agreed by the parties who typically incorporate established rules, such as the Rules of the American Arbitration Association.
Pleadings	Answer, Complaint, Counterclaims, etc. in accordance with Rules of Civil Procedure.	Brief statements submitted by the parties.
Paper discovery	All materials reasonably calculated to lead to admissible evidence.	As set forth in the applicable arbitration rules and/or permitted by the arbitrator(s).

Process Element or Procedure	Litigation	Arbitration
Depositions	Typically unlimited.	As set forth in the applicable arbitration rules and/or as permitted by the arbitrator(s).
Pretrial motions	Governed by Rule of Civil Procedure.	As set forth in the applicable arbitration rules and/or permitted by the arbitrator(s).
Admissible evidence	Governed by Federal or State rules of evidence.	Formal rules of evidence do not apply. The arbitrator may consider evidence in accordance with the applicable arbitration rules and/or as permitted by the arbitrator(s).
Trial/Hearing	Governed by Rules of Procedure, evidence, local court rules.	As determined by the arbitrator(s) subject to the due process requirements embodied in the FAA.
Confidentiality	Only if permitted by the court, and subject to First Amendment disclosures.	Yes, unless otherwise agreed by the parties.
Appeals	Generally permitted as a matter of right.	Seldom permitted.
Cost	Parties typically bear own legal fees and costs, unless a specific statute provides for cost shifting. Judges/juries are paid with public funds.	Parties may authorize arbitrator(s) to award legal fees and costs. Otherwise, parties' bear own cost and share expense of arbitrator(s).
Duration	Two to three years.	Varies but typically faster than litigation.

Efficiency Risks of Arbitration

The foregoing comparison suggests that arbitration is not inherently more or less efficient than litigation. Indeed, when the parties and the arbitrator do not manage arbitration efficiently, it can replicate litigation in most significant respects. On the other hand, arbitration provides parties with the opportunity to control the direction (and costs) of potential disputes in two critical ways: (i) by selecting an efficient arbitrator, and (ii) by setting efficient rules for arbitration in advance of a dispute.

Absent procedural constraints imposed by the parties themselves or the applicable arbitration rules, an arbitrator has more control over the dispute process than would a judge in litigation.[60] Although a judge must conform his or her procedural rulings to the governing state or federal rules, which typically provide for broad discovery as a matter of right, an arbitrator typically has discretion to permit discovery. Further, an arbitrator's discovery rulings are essentially immune from appellate review.

In view of the substantial power of an arbitrator to determine whether or not an arbitration will be conducted in a cost-efficient or wasteful manner, it is surprising that parties to a dispute often focus entirely on whether or not a proposed arbitrator has expertise in the relevant subject matter. They therefore fail to consider whether the proposed arbitrator has either a track record or established policies or practices related to dispute management. Indeed, the failure of parties to consider an arbitrator's managerial role in addition to his or her decision-making authority (and the failure of many arbitrators to manage their cases efficiently) both reduces cost savings and has led to criticism of the process as an alternative to litigation. One commentator argues:

> Both mediation and arbitration require specific skills for the impartial person or persons. For mediators, there is a particular need for the arts of listening, questioning, fact-finding, and interpreting the views of each party. The arbitrator needs all of that, plus the courtroom skills of a good judge. This starts with knowledge and experience in the rules of procedure and evidence and in substantive law. It may have to be supplemented by specialized knowledge or a firm determination to acquire the necessary learning. Arbiters should exclude bias, conflicts of interest, and personal misconduct toward the parties and their counsel. Anomalously, arbitrators who are experts or specialists in the substantive field of the dispute are seldom, if ever, impartial, but that is not ground for removal. Contrary to widespread opinion, there is no obvious match between the traits that constitute excellent judicial conduct as against those needed for arbitration or when compared with the skills appropriate for successful mediation... The skill levels, substantive experience, and personal biases of the hearing officer (arbitrator or mediator) are seldom known to the litigants at the time of their selection. ... The choice of arbitrators is essentially one of self-appointment by the candidates with little or no verification, clearance,

---

[60] (Carr & Jencks, 1999).

or appraisal. The parties seldom know the arbitrators and have no way to obtain knowledge of their skills, demeanor, bias, and reliability.[61]

Likewise, the parties to an arbitration agreement often overlook their own authority to determine their own procedures for potential disputes. Thus, the Commercial Arbitration Rules of the American Arbitration Association provide Rule R-1, entitled "Agreement of the Parties":

> The parties shall be deemed to have made these rules a part of their arbitration agreement whenever they have provided for arbitration by the American Arbitration Association (hereinafter AAA) under its Commercial Arbitration Rules or for arbitration by the AAA of a domestic commercial dispute without specifying particular rules. These rules and any amendment of them shall apply in the form in effect at the time the administrative requirements are met for a demand for arbitration or submission agreement received by the AAA. ***The parties, by written agreement, may vary the procedures set forth in these rules.*** After appointment of the arbitrator, such modifications may be made only with the consent of the arbitrator. (Emphasis added).[62]

Commonly, however, parties to arbitration agreements provide only that "disputes will be submitted for arbitration pursuant to the rules of the American Arbitration Association" or similar organizations, without consideration of their ability to customize procedures to promote efficiency. For example, the parties could consider prohibiting or expressly limiting depositions and/or prehearing motions, both of which can drastically increase dispute costs without providing corresponding improvements in the quality of information ultimately provided to the arbitrator.

In short, arbitration risks replicating the inefficiency of litigation if the parties fail to appoint an arbitrator capable of, and willing to, manage the dispute efficiently and/or if they fail to consider and plan for efficient procedures in advance of any dispute.

Efficient Options for Arbitration

Arbitration provides an exceptional opportunity for parties to resolve disputes efficiently, provided the parties plan ahead and take advantage of their ability to customize the dispute process to best fit the nature of their relationship with each other and/or the subject matter of their dealings.

---

[61] (Brown, 1997, pp. 758-760).
[62] (Commercial Arbitration Rules and Mediation Procedure).

Although the customization of the arbitration process should depend on unique circumstances of each potential dispute, the parties to an arbitration agreement might want to consider the following.

Advance Selection of an Efficient Arbitrator

Given the power of the arbitrator to determine whether or not an arbitration proceeding will be efficient, the parties should consider each arbitrator's track record and views of dispute management during the selection process. Indeed, the parties might interview prospective arbitrators to enable them to evaluate the arbitrator's ability and intentions regarding case management.

Unfortunately, it may be difficult, as a practical matter, for parties to a dispute to reach agreement on the degree to which an arbitrator should seek to control costs after a dispute has arisen. Prior to a dispute, however, all parties have strong incentives to seek an efficient dispute resolution process. Once begun, strategic factors may affect each party's preferences.[63] For example, a party with a deeper pocket may prefer a costly process, or a party that has failed to maintain good records may desire more extensive discovery than a better-prepared party.

Such strategic impediments to choosing an efficient arbitrator could be overcome by reaching agreement on an arbitrator when the arbitration agreement is negotiated. As a practical matter, predispute selection of an arbitrator might not make sense if the probability of a dispute between the parties is low, because the cost of choosing an arbitrator would outweigh the expected benefit. On the other hand, disputes are almost inevitably over certain types of agreements—such as agreements to develop information technology or construction contracts. In such instances, selection of an arbitrator in advance might result in a far more cost-effective process for resolving disputes.

Cost-Saving Procedural Rules

If the parties are unable to appoint an efficient arbitrator, they can nonetheless exercise substantial control over management of potential disputes by establishing their own procedural rules as part of their arbitration agreement. For example, the parties' arbitration agreement could control costs by restricting depositions, motions, and the duration of the entire proceeding.

---

[63] Perhaps the most notable discussion of the difference in individuals' incentives to establish fair rules before and after a conflict (or change from a position of equal negotiating power) can be found in John Rawls, "A Theory of Justice." (Rawls, 1971).

Prohibiting and/or Limiting Prehearing Motions

Because arbitration hearings are far more flexible than judicial trials, depositions are likely to be much less important in the preparation of a party's case. Further, depositions not only increase the direct costs of a dispute by virtue of attorney time, court reporter fees, etc., that they entail, they are also likely to create inefficient use of resources and redundancies.

Depositions can be wasteful for several reasons. First, the examining attorney has far less incentive to focus on directly relevant, material information than at a trial or hearing. To the contrary, a deposition is an ideal opportunity for a "fishing expedition" because unproductive questions and answers can simply be ignored.

Second, participants in a deposition are typically required to attend the trial or hearing to replicate relevant testimony.

Third, depositions are often relied upon to create a record for pretrial motions. Because, as discussed below, pretrial motions, such as motions for summary judgment and motions to exclude evidence, rarely make sense in arbitration proceedings, a significant need for depositions is absent.

Fourth, depositions for purposes of an arbitration may, in many cases, be more costly that pretrial depositions. The FAA and state laws do not expressly provide for subpoenas to compel witness attendance at a deposition (although they do provide subpoena power to compel attendance at arbitration hearings). Consequently, the parties may need to incur significant costs to persuade a court to compel a witness to attend a deposition prior to an arbitration hearing.

Prohibit and/or Limit Prehearing Motions

In litigation, motions on pleadings and motions for summary judgment are frequently submitted to obtain dismissal of an action or to limit the scope of issues for trial. Although prehearing motions could serve the same role in arbitration, they are far more likely to increase the costs of a dispute than to succeed or otherwise streamline the dispute.

Substantive prehearing motions are unlikely to succeed in arbitration because arbitrators have a strong incentive to hear evidence and arguments at a hearing rather than to exclude them in advance. In fact, one of the few grounds for overturning an arbitrator's award is for "refusing to hear evidence pertinent and material to the controversy."[64] As a result, it is far easier (and far more likely) for an arbitrator to deny prehearing motions than to grant them.

Further, prehearing motions often lead to redundant submissions of materials and responses before and during the hearing. Although pretrial

---

[64] 9 U.S.C. § 10.

motions are often submitted to "educate" the judge (or arbitrator) about a party's views, rather than to succeed, such education may carry a significant cost.

Similarly, prehearing evidentiary motions—called "motions *in limine*"— are unlikely to be cost-justified in an arbitration proceeding. Motions to exclude evidence play an important role in litigation, because they allow the parties and the court to decide in advance upon the scope of evidence that a jury will be permitted to hear. In arbitration, the arbitrator will hear the disputed evidence in any event—either in ruling on the motion *in limine* or at the hearing. Although a motion *in limine* may affect the weight an arbitrator gives to disputed evidence, the parties are free to address this issue at the hearing in any event. Consequently, as with substantive prehearing motions, the cost of evidentiary motions is unlikely to outweigh their benefits.

Setting Time Limits for Completion of the Arbitration

As part of their arbitration agreement, the parties could impose reasonable time limits on themselves and the arbitrator for completion of the arbitration. Even if the parties permitted the arbitrator to extend the deadlines in the event of a force majeure event or good cause, an agreed upon timetable promotes efficiency for two reasons. First, and perhaps most importantly, experience suggests that the amount of legal work (and fees) generated by a dispute expands to meet the allotted time. Second, a timetable provides the parties with a better ability to plan (and budget) for the dispute.

Conclusion

Properly managed, arbitration has significant potential to reduce the costs of disputes while providing high-quality decisions. Further, by eliminating the "luck of draw" in court, arbitration can provide the parties with confidence that they will be heard, understood, and treated fairly.

CHAPTER VII: *Models for Efficient Resolution of Business Disputes: Investigatory Mediation and Arbitration and Co-Expert Mediation*

Business disputes may be resolved at a far lower cost than through litigation by eliminating potentially wasteful redundancy in the decision-making process. This chapter suggests two innovative methods to eliminate wasteful redundancy in dispute resolution, while improving the quality of decision-making or the fairness of agreed resolutions. As explained in this chapter, the same straightforward procedures for eliminating redundancy have the potential to improve the quality of decision-making by transforming the decision maker from a passive observer with a possibly limited personal investment in the process into an active investigator charged by all parties with the duty to elicit impartially the relevant facts and determine the dispute in accordance with applicable law. Alternatively, the parties can deploy dispute resolution and subject matter experts in an efficient collaborative manner, rather than effectively waste these costly resources in combative and destructive litigation.

Investigatory Mediation and Arbitration

The first proposed dispute resolution process, which I have named "Investigatory Mediation and Arbitration," or "IMA," has the potential to cut dispute resolution cost dramatically—possibly by as much as 75 or 80 percent when compared with litigation—and to improve the quality of the resulting determinations. Although the quality of an adjudicatory decision is impossible to measure objectively, it is reasonable to assume that the quality of decision-making depends on (i) the qualification and experience of the decision maker; (ii) the quality—in terms of relevance and completeness—of the information considered by the decision maker, and (iii) the level of attention and time devoted by the decision maker to resolution of disputed issues of fact and law.

In simplest form, IMA may be implemented as follows:

1.   The parties jointly select an Investigatory Neutral based upon his or her suitability (in terms of expertise and experience) for efficient

Investigatory Mediation and Arbitration ("IMA")

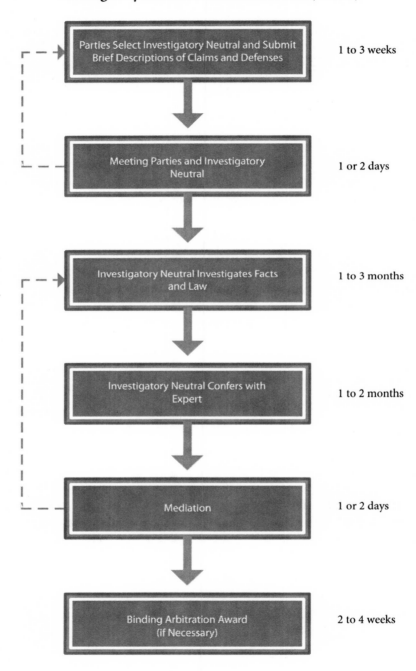

understanding and resolution of the dispute. (Selection could be made using any of the well-established processes for selection of a single arbitrator or mediator.)

2. The parties (and their legal counsel) meet with the Investigatory Neutral to specify the issues in dispute and their respective claims and counterclaims.

3. The Investigatory Neutral independently researches applicable law and initiates fact finding by requiring the production of documents and interviewing or deposing witnesses. When necessary, the Investigatory Neutral initiates and subpoenas witnesses to attend one or more arbitration hearings to allow testimony and documents to be elicited from third parties. (Any party or nonparty witness is permitted to have counsel present during examination by the Investigatory Neutral.) The parties are free to discuss/negotiate the scope of discovery with the Investigatory Neutral to allow for discovery focused on the issues deemed important to the Investigatory Neutral.

4. If necessary, the Investigatory Neutral retains one or more "experts" to provide assistance with complex or technical factual issues.

5. The party representatives with full settlement authority (and their legal counsel) meet with the Investigatory Neutral to discuss the Investigatory Neutral's preliminary findings and conclusions and to attempt to settle the dispute via the Investigatory Neutral's evaluative mediation. The parties may also suggest additional areas of inquiry for the Investigatory Neutral (if the dispute is not resolved).

6. If necessary, steps 3 through 5 may be repeated.

7. Failing a negotiated resolution, the Investigatory Neutral issues a binding arbitration award.

The IMA model offers the following cost savings (when compared to litigation).

- Elimination of redundant fact finding by the parties.
- Reduction of duplicative legal research.
- Avoidance of wasteful discovery disputes and posturing. (Obviously, the parties may refuse to comply with the arbitrator's discovery requests at their own peril.)
- Avoidance of duplicative but often discounted expert testimony.
- Elimination of repetition of witness testimony as discovery and the "hearing" of the matter are effectively merged.

- Promotion of settlement agreement by providing clarity as to the rules governing the dispute in a timely matter.

My concept of IMA is intended to reduce the cost of resolving complex disputes both by reducing redundant information gathering and presentation by the parties, and by providing the parties with timely information about the rules that will ultimately determine the allocation of liabilities and recoveries. By allowing interactions between the parties and the Investigatory Neutral, the parties are able to ascertain the "rules" well in advance of an award by the Investigatory Neutral and certainly without the extraordinary expense of learning them only via a court or jury's award. Once the parties know the rules governing their dispute, their ability to reach sensible and efficient resolutions increase dramatically.

Indeed, one key reason that many cases settle "on the courthouse steps," or even after trial has begun, is that the litigation process often provides little guidance to the parties as to rules (*i.e.*, legal principles) that will govern the dispute until shortly before the trial begins. Although some legal rulings may be obtained via motions on the pleading or summary judgment, key legal rulings are often left to the eve of trial. For example, rulings on the evidence that will be permitted or excluded from trial, jury instructions, and similar matters commonly await the trial itself, regardless of the potential for significantly altering the parties' assessments of their claims and defense.

The proposed model, moreover, encourages mediation, because it eliminates the risk that the cost of educating and interacting with a mediator might be wasted. In traditional models, a common objection to mediation and arbitration by a single Neutral is that his or her arbitration decision might be tainted by confidential information learned from one or the other party in mediation. Conversely, the parties might understandably be reluctant to share information with a mediator that could be used against them at an arbitration hearing.

By contrast, mediation by an Investigatory Neutral does not depend on the information to be shared by the parties during a day of mediation, but instead centers on the Investigatory Neutral's preliminary conclusions respecting the relevant facts and law. In this more evaluative model of mediation, the goal is to assist the parties to understand factors likely to affect a final resolution and thereby help them reach a common assessment of the "settlement value" of the case. In addition, the Investigatory Neutral assists the parties to explore mutually beneficial means of creating value (or reducing their respective costs) to further facilitate a negotiated settlement.

IMA improves the quality of decision-making because it not only promotes selection of a well-qualified Investigatory Neutral, but also provides incentives for him or her to explore and understand the potentially complex facts and law. The Investigatory Neutral becomes an expert in the dispute itself and relies upon that expertise to encourage settlement or, if necessary, decide the matter or unresolved parts of the dispute. Indeed, by dramatically reducing the cost of the process, IMA encourages settlements based upon a just allocation of rights and liabilities (coupled with possible agreements to create value for the parties) rather than settlements forced upon one or another party simply by virtue of the cost and uncertainty of litigation.

Because the concept of IMA departs from the adversarial advocacy that underlies traditional common law means of resolving disputes, it undoubtedly raises eyebrows and doubts.

For example, businesses may be reluctant to cede control over the dispute process to an independent investigator/arbitrator. However, such an argument assumes that, by contrast, litigation affords a party meaningful control. Indeed, other than the ability of a party's litigation counsel to use (or misuse) discovery and to posture through motions practice, IMA arguably affords the parties far more meaningful control over a dispute by allowing them to select the adjudicator instead of gambling on the draws of judge and jury.

More significantly, parties might be concerned that an Investigatory Neutral will not as aggressively ferret out the facts and truth from an adversary. The effectiveness of an Investigatory Neutral's investigation doubtless varies (just as the effectiveness of parties' counsel may vary). On the other hand, and even if an Investigatory Neutral pursues an adversary less aggressively than a party's own counsel, it seems unlikely that the dramatically greater cost of the adversarial litigation process is justified by the prospects for marginally greater aggressiveness.

Finally, the "due process" ramifications of IMA need to be considered. In the adversary system, the hallmarks of due process are the right to be heard and to cross-examine adverse witnesses. Whether a model that replaces traditional concepts of due process with one grounded in the parties' consent to an efficient resolution would be accepted and/or enforced remains to be examined and tested.

In short, IMA merits consideration because of its exceptional potential for efficiency, especially when viewed in light of the systemic wastefulness of traditional litigation. Of course, parties do not always choose litigation in the hopes of achieving an efficient and just resolution of a dispute. A party may perceive the inefficiency of the process as a tactical advantage or hope for an irrational judgment to save a weak case. IMA may, however, provide a sensible ADR option for parties seeking to resolve a business dispute in good faith.

Co-Expert Mediation

Closely related to IMA, but more akin to traditional dispute resolution methods, is a process I have named Co-Expert Mediation or "CEM." CEM recognizes that achieving agreement between or among disputing parties typically requires two forms of expertise: expertise in dispute resolution and in the subject matter at issue. Although professional mediators often believe in, and tout, their ability to resolve disputes of any kind and sometime suggest that lack of subject matter expertise is preferable (because it seemingly affords the parties with greater control over their own resolution),[65] businesses seeking mediation of complex disputes typically disagree. Surveys and studies of parties to complex business disputes routinely conclude that subject matter expertise is the most important qualification of a mediator.[66]

Unfortunately, expertise in dispute resolution and subject matter expertise may not go hand-in-hand. Further, a subject matter expert, such as an economist, business value expert, IT professional, engineer, etc., may be reluctant to serve as the sole mediator of a dispute because of concern that his or her objective insights may appear biased to a party or due to lack of familiarity with the mediation process itself.

The efficient solution provided by CEM, therefore, is to provide for co-mediation administered by an expert in dispute resolution with the involvement of one or more subject matter experts. The subject matter expert could then freely interact with both parties and promote efforts to reduce the gap between the parties' likely biased perceptions of key facts (and the interpretation of those facts) and objective reality.

CEM may increase the short-run cost of mediation by requiring the services of more than a single neutral, but the long-run savings from CEM can be exceptional. As explained in Chapter III, redundant expert witnesses greatly contribute to the overall expense of litigation. Not only must experts (like legal counsel) replicate their own efforts two or three time during a case, but also competing (and redundant and biased expert witnesses) may simply cancel each other out during a trial before a jury that may not be capable of fully understanding either side's presentation. By deploying a neutral expert focused

---

[65] (Roberts & Jessica, 2005).

[66] (American Bar Association, Section of Dispute Resolution, 2008, p. 9)("To a very substantial degree, users [of mediation] endorsed the importance of subject matter knowledge, and in complex cases, subject matter expertise may be prefered")(Thomson, 2001) (discussing survey of construction law counsel).

on reducing the gap between the parties' respective appraisals, the parties can achieve both substantial savings and higher quality and better reasoned outcomes.

CHAPTER VIII: Dispute Containment and Management of Project Disputes

In a perfect business relationship (or a perfect world), costs for disputes are nonexistent, because there would be no disputes. Disputes, however, are not only inevitable; in some circumstances they are entirely predictable. Just as preventative healthcare or routine equipment maintenance can avoid far greater costs in the future, planning for disputes and managing business relationships with the risk of disputes in mind can go a long way to minimizing costly legal battles.

Although there are a variety of methods for managing potential disputes, they essentially rest on a single principle: businesses should strive to resolve disputes promptly as a means of keeping small disputes small, rather than allowing them to fester and transform themselves into corporate wars.

The simple concept of containing disputes is more difficult than it sounds for two reasons. First, the parties must have mechanisms in place to identify and quickly resolve problems as they arise. Such mechanisms can, and should be, included in any complex transaction or engagement that requires the parties to interact over a period of time—such as a construction project or software development agreement. Second, the parties must actually deploy the mechanisms they have agreed upon.

Perhaps surprisingly, the second requisite—use of available dispute mechanisms—is where parties to a business arrangement often fall short. Once a project is underway, the parties to a business arrangement often prefer to focus exclusively on moving forward and "working things out" as they proceed with each other. Further, the individuals implementing a project may be a completely different group of people than those who negotiated the arrangement (and any dispute resolution mechanism). Indeed, project personnel may never even look at the contract terms governing their relationship, preferring instead to relegate "legal issues" to the back burner.

The problem with assuming that problems will work themselves out is that they often do not. Further, issues or problems with complex projects seldom arise alone, but typically arise in groups or a series. As a result, when a series of small issues are not addressed, the project itself may take on a character that is quite distinct from the project originally contemplated by the parties who negotiated the terms of the relationship. If the parties have not addressed and modified their contract expectations along the way when the series of small issues emerges as an unworkable mess, the cost of untangling the parties' respective duties and obligations can be extraordinary.

Managing Potential Disputes with Effective Contracts

The starting point for managing potential risks is to negotiate contracts that both clearly articulate the parties' respective obligations and specify efficient procedures for resolving disagreements as they arise.

In defining the parties' obligations, an effective contract addresses the fact that the parties may have multiple types of relationships with each other in a single transaction. For example, when a business hires a software developer to create new inventory software, it may need to rely on the vendor for a variety of services in addition to development of the software itself. The business may, for example, require customization of the software to assure its compatibility with other software and systems; the conversion of existing data files to allow effective operation of the new system; the development of specialized features, functions, or interfaces; or system maintenance and support, including periodic upgrades or enhancements to meet changing business or regulatory requirements. Each service or component of the deal should be analyzed separately because a misunderstanding or deficiency in any area could undermine the entire transaction and give rise to a costly dispute.

Not only should a contract identify the different types of relationships the parties create, it should clearly articulate their respective rights and obligations if their respective performances fall short of expectations. In other words, the parties must address who is responsible, and to what extent, if the goods or services delivered under the arrangement fail to work properly, do not work at all, or are not delivered on time.

Managing Disputes as They Arise

Businesses frequently seek legal advice when entering into agreements and when disputes arise. The same companies, however, often overlook the role of sound legal practice in monitoring and managing the implementation of their agreements. The effective management of implementation can prevent costly disputes or improve a party's likelihood of success should a dispute become unavoidable. Managing problems as they arise has three main elements.

First, the parties must decide who bears responsibility for the problem. This can be difficult. Did the problem arise because the supplier overstated the capabilities of it product? Did the purchaser incorrectly specify its requirements? Did problems arise due to personnel changes at either the purchaser or vendor? Or did the problem arise because external facts, such as governmental regulations, economic conditions, or technologies, have changed.

Second, the parties should agree on a timetable for curing the defect or problem.

Third, the parties should agree on a remedy if the problem is not resolved in the specified period. Remedies might include project termination, fee reduction, or concessions on other matters.

All agreements regarding changes in the project or remedies for problems should be in writing. A clear demarcation of rights and responsibilities almost certainly promotes effective management of the project and reduces the risk of protracted disputes later on. By contrast, failure to address significant problems can allow them to fester and grow.

Managing Project Disputes

Escalating Negotiations

Perhaps the most common form of managing project disputes is the requirement of escalating negotiations. Parties plan for disputes by including in their contract a requirement that, in advance of litigation or other processes involving third parties, the parties first try to resolve disputes through negotiation at escalating managerial levels.

Such agreements, for example, may require each party to designate a project lead or manager who has front line responsibility for formal communications and notices during the course of the project. Further, the contract may specify that, prior to initiating litigation or arbitration, a party must first bring the matter to the attention of the other party's project manager and then attempt to negotiate a resolution within a specified period, such as two weeks. The contract may further require that, in the event the managers fail to negotiate a resolution, the parties must escalate the matter to one or more higher levels of management for one or more additional rounds of negotiation. Effective escalation requirements will, moreover, typically require the parties to enter written amendments or change orders to formalize any negotiated resolutions.

Escalation is perhaps most effective for managing disputes between parties that have long standing and/or multifaceted relationships. In such cases, while front line managers may have the best information about the specific project or dispute in question, high-level managers may have a better understanding of the range of relationships between the parties and/or potential tradeoffs involving matters outside the scope of the project giving rise to the dispute.

Escalation requirements, however, are not riskless or appropriate to all business arrangements. In some instances, such requirements may delay resolution without increasing the likelihood of a settlement. Because of a lack of day-to-day project involvement, senior managers may lack sufficient information or perspective about projects to fairly evaluate the dispute and, therefore, may adopt unproductive negotiating positions.

Further, and perhaps more significantly, an escalation provision may prevent, rather than promote, efficient resolution of disputes because of reluctance by one or another of the parties to involve senior managers in matters that might reflect poorly on the front line managers themselves or others working on the project. In other words, instead of serving to promote prompt resolution of disputes, escalation clauses sometime create incentives to sweep problems under the rug until they grow so large that they become unmanageable.

Appointment of a "Project Neutral"

In addition to bilateral processes for managing and containing disputes, it may make sense in some instances for the parties jointly to retain a "project neutral" to mediate and possibly even arbitrate disputes as they arise during the course of the project or business relationship.

There are several significant benefits to the appointment of a neutral in advance of potential business disputes: First, as noted in the prior chapter, it is likely far easier for the parties to agree upon a neutral who has both knowledge of the subject matter of the business relationship and a commitment to minimize dispute costs prior to the onset of conflict between the parties. At the outset of the business relationship, both parties have incentive to minimize the cost of potential disputes and, assuming good faith, neither is likely to have the upper hand.

Second, appointing a neutral in advance, and establishing agreed upon procedures for resolving disputes, decreases the start-up cost of seeking assistance to resolve a dispute and makes it more likely that the parties will act quickly to address problems as they arise. Not only can the dispute be initiated without delays for the selection of the neutral, but it would also eliminate some of the time necessary to educate the neutral about the nature of the project, the terms of the contract, etc. (assuming that the neutral is provided periodic updates on the status of the project).

Controlling Dispute Costs

Despite best efforts, some disputes are unavoidable. In such cases, a party can best manage its own potential costs of the dispute by acting quickly to prepare for litigation or other dispute resolution processes. A party should, for example:

- Collect relevant technical and legal documents, including all correspondence with the other party.
- Interview project personnel.
- Prepare a chronology that describes the history of dealings between the parties.
- Fairly evaluate the strengths and weaknesses of potential claims.
- Assess potential litigation costs as part of evaluating settlement posture.
- Consider various mechanisms for resolving the dispute, including direct negotiation, mediation, arbitration, and litigation.

In addition to evaluating the available evidence, a party to a potential dispute must recognize that continued dealings with the other party will have legal significance. Because the record of dealings between the parties may be murky, the manner in which the parties discuss a dispute may itself affect the outcome. As a consequence, a party to a potential dispute should identify the legal and factual basis for its position and should refrain from conduct that could be construed as inconsistent with that position.

To mitigate damages, for example, once a decision has been made to terminate an agreement, the termination should be done quickly to avoid the accumulation of additional damages or business injury. The party purchasing the services should consider appointing someone to manage all continued communication with the opposing party to avoid sending conflicting messages. The person in charge of such communications should work closely with legal counsel to promote a consistent and effective legal posture for the dispute.

Finally, a party to a business dispute should coordinate its business and legal strategies. Given the uncertainty inherent in legal proceedings involving complex matters, a party should not rely solely on legal proceedings to resolve its strategic business concerns.

CHAPTER IX: *Dispute Management Systems: Case Studies and Cost Savings*

Over the past 20 years, many leading corporations and government agencies have come to realize the savings and benefits to be achieved by the adoption of policies, protocols, and/or systems that address disputes proactively and efficiently. Effective dispute management systems not only have the ability to save extraordinary levels of resources, they can also improve morale, productivity, and effective collaboration.

Perhaps because of organizational barriers to the development and implementation of dispute management systems, such systems have tended to develop piecemeal within large organizations. For example, a company may establish a policy of mediation and/or arbitration for disputes with contractors, but maintain outdated grievance procedures for employees. Healthcare organizations may adopt ADR to address disputes with patients but not internal disputes among staff, and so on. More often than not, the impetus for developing a system to manage disputes is a crisis, exploding legal fees, and/or a particularly bad outcome in litigation. For example, an Assistant General Counsel for Johnson & Johnson noted that the company's increasing spending on outside counsel fees and an $11 million adverse ruling prodded it to becoming more aggressive in developing an ADR program.[67] Similarly, Halliburton's in-house labor counsel for twenty years explains:

> Beginning in 1992, it became clear to me that there was something inherently wrong with the litigation process as it was applied to employment cases. Like most major companies, Halliburton won most of the employment cases filed against it or settled the claims for modest amounts. The amounts we spent on outside lawyers exceeded several times what we paid in settlements. However, the money Halliburton spent for the privilege of winning most of its cases had little tangible impact on the Company or its employees. ...

---

[67] (How Companies Manage Employment Disputes: A Compendium of Leading Employment Programs, 2002).

What brought about the real need for change in the process was a sexual harassment and tort claim trial which took place in 1992... The case had been around ... for almost five years by the time it reached trial. [Halliburton] obtained favorable verdicts... However, the case cost almost $450,000 in legal fees, and permanently altered the careers of several employees and former employees, including the plaintiff.... The financial and human cost associated with that kind of litigation was so high that we began a concerted effort to examine alternatives.[68]

This chapter will review the development, implementation, and beneficial consequences of several notable dispute management systems.

Comprehensive Dispute Management: The United States Air Force

The United States Air Force has been a leader (if not an evangelist) promoting the use of ADR to resolve both workplace and commercial disputes. The Air Force was one of the first federal agencies to use ADR; it began in 1989 with equal employment opportunity ("EEO") complaints. Since that time, it has expanded its program to include all types of disputes, including negotiated and administrative grievances, unfair labor practice charges, Merit System Protection Board appeals, and contracting matters. The Air Force has itself trained more than 1,500 mediators, including EEO counselors, personnel specialists, and management and union officials.

The Air Force's use of ADR—especially mediation—to resolve workplace disputes has been both impressive and well documented. While statistical and financial data comparing ADR with traditional dispute resolution methods is typically sparse, the Air Force has consistently attempted to measure the benefits of its broad programs. Based on its own and additional government data from the 1990s, the Air Force drew a range conclusions about the cost of litigation and the savings derived from ADR.

For example, by breaking litigation costs down into discrete elements, the Air Force showed the level of savings that can be achieved through early resolution. The Air Force identified the following costs of EEO complaints based on data from 1988 (which was then converted to cost estimates for 1999).

---

[68] (Bedman).

	1988 Costs	1999 Costs
PreComplaint..	822.78	
Counseling..	1,360.03	
Filed Formal..	787.08	
Investigation..	3,213.44	
Post Investigation with Resolution....................	2,231.12	
Proposed Disposition..................................	2,854.90	
Final Agency Decision Without Hearing..............	1,521.00	
Hearing..	6,041.20	
Final Agency Decision After EEOC Hearing............	2,281.50	
SUBTOTAL..	21,113.05	28,872
Settlements..	15,537.00	21,264
SUBTOTAL..		50,136
Appeal..		136,083
Indirect Costs of Final Processing of a Case ($8,000.00)***..............		$14,390
Total estimate..		$200,609

In addition, the Air Force noted that in fiscal year 1994, 84% of all EEO discrimination complaints that entered into their ADR process achieved a complete settlement; partial settlements pushed this success rate to nearly 90%, with a 100% compliance rate.[69]

Further, surveys show that most of the Air Force personnel who used ADR techniques to settle their disputes were either very satisfied or satisfied. In fiscal year 1994, 99.6% of the complainants who used ADR and settled their case within 30 days reported that they would use it again; 98.3% who settled their cases through ADR between 30 and 60 days reported that they would use it again, and 100% of all the other participants who settled their cases in over 60 days reported that they would try ADR again.

---

[69] (United States Air Force, 2002).

These statistics from the mid-1990s were reaffirmed in 2005 and 2006.[70] In those years, the Air Force's workplace ADR showed the following results:

Early Resolution (ER) Attempt and Resolution
Rates in Workplace Disputes, FY 05 - FY 06

	FY 2005[*]	FY 2006
Total Workplace Disputes	6281	6200
Early Resolution (ER) Attempts	3414	3137
Early Resolutions	2628	2496
Total ER Attempt Rate	54%	51%
Total ER Resolution Rate	77%	80%

According to the Air Force's EEO statistical report for 2006:

- In informal precomplaints, ADR was offered in 910 of the 1348 cases processed, an offer rate of 67%. Of these offers, 477, or 52%, were accepted.
- Of the 477 informal precomplaints that went to ADR, 321, or 67%, were successfully resolved.
- In formal complaints, ADR was offered in 299 of 1148 cases processed, an offer rate of only 26%. Of these offers, 157, or 53%, were accepted.
- Of the 157 formal complaints that went to ADR, 129, or 82%, were successfully resolved.

Equally important, the workplace dispute procedures were viewed favorably by the great majority of participants.

ADR Customer Satisfaction FY 06

Process	Very Satisfied	Satisfied	Neutral	Dissatisfied	Very Dissatisfied
	67%	21%	8%	3%	1%
Neutral	Excellent	Good	Average	Fair	Poor
	84%	14%	2%	0%	0%

With respect to contracting, the Air Force has entered into agreements with 17 of its largest suppliers to use ADR before resorting to litigation. While there is some variation in the wording used in these corporate agreements,

---

[70] (Air Force Instruction 36-1201, 2007).

each of them essentially commits the parties to use ADR, in lieu of litigation, to facilitate resolution. The Air Force, for example, entered into program-level ADR agreements covering most of its major weapon system contracts.

Contractors and weapons suppliers entering ADR agreements with the Air Force include:

Bechtel National, Inc.	ARAAM (Raytheon)
United Technologies Corporation	AWACS (Boeing)
GTE Government Systems	AWACS (Plexsys)
Lockheed Martin Corporation	B-1 (Boeing)
Harris Corporation	B2 (NG) (2)
Northrop Grumman Corporation	C- 17 (Boeing)
Alliant Techsystems Inc.	C- 17 ATS (Boeing)
TRW Inc.	F- 15 Boeing
Sverdrup Corporation	C-130 AMP (Boeing)
DynCorp	Delta IV (Boeing) & Atlas V (LM)
The Boeing Company	F-15 (MD Boeing)

Science Application International Corporation	F-15 (NG)
ITT Industries, Defense & Electronics	F-16 (LM)
Raytheon Company, Inc.	F-16 Radar (NG)
Tracor Aerospace, Inc.	GCSS (LM)
Litton Industries Inc.	General Overarching Principles
GE Aircraft Engines	(Boeing)
AlliedSignal Inc.	JASSM (LM)
	JDAM
	JSF F35 (LM)
	JSTARS (NG)
	MALD
	MILSATCO (Boeing)
	MILSATCOM (LM)
	MILSATCOM EHF EMD (LM)
	Network (Honeywell)
	PREDATOR (General Atomics)
	SBIRS (LM)
	SBIRS DSP (NG Revision)
	SBIRS DSP (NG)
	SDB (Boeing)
	Space Radar (LM)
	Space Radar (TRW)
	WCMD AND SFW

The Air Force's basic ADR agreement is as follows:

Statement of Principles Regarding the Use of
Alternative Dispute Resolution Processes
Between
The Department of the Air Force
and

_____

The Department of the Air Force (Air Force) and _____ share the objective of supplying America's war fighters with technologically advanced and reliable equipment in a timely manner to promote swift, safe and successful accomplishment of the national defense mission. Litigation unnecessarily consumes scarce and expensive resources and detracts from this mission. For most disputes, Alternative Dispute Resolution (ADR) is a less expensive and more effective method of resolution than the traditional legal remedies. ADR procedures involve collaborative techniques which can spare both the Air Force and _____ the expenses and burdens of litigation.

In recognition of the foregoing, we affirm our commitment to use ADR processes by agreeing to the following principles. We agree to:

- Conduct our business in a manner that will avoid or minimize disputes.

- Utilize a cooperative philosophy throughout the acquisition life cycle. In furtherance of this principle, all Air Force/_____ teams are encouraged to conduct a joint review of the contract's goals and objectives, identify potential obstacles to the contract's timely and effective completion, and periodically assess progress toward overcoming these obstacles.

- Resolve all contract issues at the lowest possible level. This principle recognizes that: 1) the detailed knowledge of the issues is generally at the program level; and, 2) the resolution of problems at that level fosters teamwork in pursuing mutually satisfactory solutions.

- In the event an issue cannot be resolved through negotiation, the parties shall, in lieu of litigation, endeavor to use ADR to facilitate resolution. Air Force and _____ management will be kept advised of progress in resolving these issues, whether through negotiation or through ADR techniques.

- Consistent with FAR 33.214, the Air Force and _____ will, before initiation of the use of ADR for a particular matter, agree in writing to specific ADR collaborative techniques, timelines and identification of neutrals appropriate to the issues in controversy.

- If it is necessary for the parties to protect information during the ADR process, the parties will enter into a confidentiality agreement sufficient to maintain such information in confidence to the extent permitted by law.

- It is not the intention of the parties for this agreement to alter, supplement or deviate from the terms and conditions of contract(s) between the parties and the legal rights and obligations of the parties set forth therein. Any changes to the contract(s) must be executed in writing by authorized contracting officials.

- In the event either party believes a particular issue is not well-suited to ADR, or is dissatisfied with progress being made in a particular ADR proceeding, that party may, after good faith efforts to resolve the issue, elect to opt out of the ADR processes and proceed as otherwise provided under contract, regulation or statute. Nothing in this Statement of Principles shall prevent either party from preserving its legal rights and remedies during the ADR process.[71]

Although the Air Force's model agreement is "soft" in the sense of not imposing ADR with agreement in advance of a dispute, it has been both popular and successful. As shown in the following tables, ADR was used in the great majority of disputes for which it was proposed and its use resulted in dramatically shorter (and therefore far less expensive) disputes than litigated actions.

---

[71] (United States Air Force).

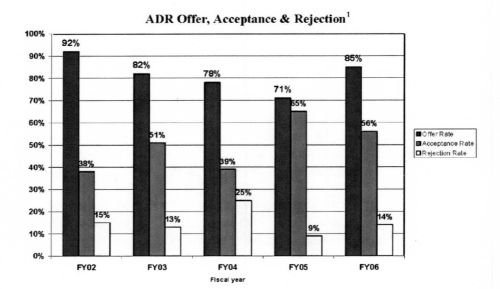

ADR Offer, Acceptance & Rejection[1]

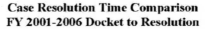

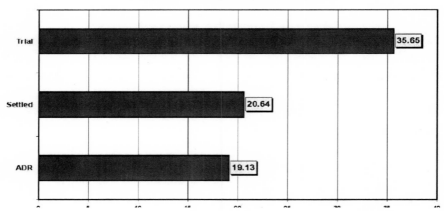

Case Resolution Time Comparison
FY 2001-2006 Docket to Resolution

Commercial and Product Liability Disputes: Georgia-Pacific and The Toro Company

Two companies that have reported significant success in reducing litigation expense through ADR are Georgia-Pacific, a Fortune 500 manufacturer of tissue, pulp, paper, packaging, building products, and related chemicals, and The Toro Company, a manufacturer of turf maintenance equipment and precision irrigation systems. Like the U.S. Air Force, based on their experiences, both companies are proponents of ADR and have shared their experiences with industry groups.[72][73]

Georgia-Pacific's counsel for litigation and ADR has described the origins of the company's program as follows:

> ...[Georgia-Pacific's interest in ADR began] when James F. Kelley took over as Georgia-Pacific's senior vice president and general counsel in December of 1993. Analyzing the company's caseload, he realized that Georgia-Pacific entered into settlements for amounts that could have been reasonably estimated much earlier in the process, even before any significant discovery had been undertaken. He deemed it more sensible to settle for that amount or perhaps even less early in the process to save the legal fees and costs (including the time of company employees) that would otherwise be incurred in defending the suit. As part of an ongoing. corporate-wide cost-cutting effort. Kelley incorporated his thinking about early case evaluation into an overhaul of the legal department. Rather than the standard pyramid, Kelley's philosophy' was to flatten out his staff and move away from a department in which lawyers manage other lawyers. Attorneys were required to be practitioners, to do more in-house and to become less reliant on outside counsel. Additionally, he required his staff to become actively involved in each case, as opposed to just monitoring the performance of outside counsel, and set up a separate litigation group to manage all the company's lawsuits. Early case evaluation, emphasizing ADR was mandated for virtually every suit filed against the company.[74]

Georgia-Pacific's program to manage the cost of its dispute has two main elements: (i) dedication and training of its legal personnel to evaluate cases for ADR and to participate in ADR process and (ii) like the Air Force, to enter ADR agreements with is suppliers and customers. Over the years, Georgia-Pacific has used a variety of dispute management agreements, including two-, three-, and even four-step processes involving one or two stages of negotiation, mediation, and arbitration.

---

[72] Georgia-Pacific's Counsel for Litigation and ADR, Philip M. Armstrong, has tracked the history and success of its program in a series of articles. *See* (Armstrong, CASE Study: Georgia-Pacific's Aggressive Use of Early Case Evaluation and ADR, 1998) (Armstrong, Georgia-Pacific's ADR Program: A Critical Review After 10 Years, 2005).

[73] Donald S. Trevarthen, Director, Division Counsel of The Toro Company, has likewise shared his company's experience in seminars and presentations. Information contained herein is taken from his Powerpoint presentation entitled, "Toro's Alternative Dispute Resolution Program Handling Product Liability Claims and Lawsuits." (Trevarthen)

[74] Armstrong (1998).

Although Georgia-Pacific initially included arbitration as the final dispute resolution stage in its ADR agreements, it later opted to remove this provision—allowing the parties instead to choose litigation (the default) or arbitration if negotiations failed. This change was apparently made, in part, because Georgia-Pacific concluded that the prospects of costly litigation helped encourage settlements. In a 1999 article, Mr. Armstrong explained:

> At first glance, it seems ideal to move disputants into increasingly structured environments until resolution is finally achieved. But ADR clauses that incorporate all three steps may actually hinder the prospects of reaching a satisfactory result. Indeed, too often the arbitration step undermines the rest of the process. The first two steps, negotiation and mediation, are most likely to lead to settlement when the only alternative is costly and time-consuming litigation. With arbitration as a viable option, the parties tend not to negotiate or mediate with the same sense of urgency or purpose, making settlement less likely.[75]

Georgia-Pacific has reported substantial savings from its emphasis on early case evaluation and ADR in its commercial disputes. In 1996, the company resolved nearly 50 cases without litigation. In 1997, the number of such cases increased to 74, resulting in estimated savings of $6.5 million.[76] After 10 years, the company found that their estimated savings were approximately $32 million in nearly 600 cases, or about $54,000 per case.[77]

The Toro Company began its ADR program in the early 1990s to address product liability claims. As a manufacturer of lawn mowers and the like, such claims may be inevitable for Toro. Toro's ADR program seeks to supplant

---

[75] (Armstrong, 1999) Although the prospect of costly litigation may encourage settlements, it may not necessarily encourage equitable ones based on the merits of the underlying disputes. Where negotiation/mediation is conducted under a cloud of litigation, the outcome may be distorted by the parties' respective ability to withstand and/or inflict such costs on each other. On one hand, the party with the deeper pocket may be able to extract an unduly favorable settlement simply by virtue of the other party's greater fear of the potential cost. On the other hand, the smaller party may be able to threaten a greater infliction of litigation costs on the other party through discovery and the like. (For example, and an individual or small business may be able to respond to document requests in discovery with little or no cost, while a multinational company may face extraordinary costs to respond to such discovery).

[76] (Armstrong, 1998), *supra.*

[77] To minimize risks of nuisance or repeat lawsuits, Georgia-Pacific aggressively litigates claims that are unlikely to be resolved through negotiation such as frivolous claims based on its deep pockets, or in cases where an overriding principle or precedent-setting issue is at stake. Even with its effective ADR strategies, Georgia-Pacific still litigates more cases than it mediates. (Armstrong, 2005)

litigation entirely as the means for addressing product-related matters with its customers. Toro's program emphasizes three steps: (1) Prevention, through safety programs, education and the like; (2) Early intervention and investigation of claims; and (3) Prelitigation mediation.

The second step of Toro's program focuses on solving its customers' problems rather than posturing for litigation. Toro describes the elements of this stage as including an onsite investigation by personnel including a Toro engineer, interviews, creating a photographic and documentary record of the accident, and expressing courtesy and concern for the claimant. After evaluation of the information, Toro shares its information with the claimant and his/her counsel and attempts to negotiate a fair resolution. Toro settles two-thirds of the claims through negotiation. The remaining cases are referred to mediation, where 95% of the remaining claims settle.

Toro has described the success of its program in glowing terms. According to a recent article:

> About 1,400 products liability claims were handled through Toro's ADR program since its inception, said Andrew R. Byers, senior manager, corporate product integrity for Toro, based in Bloomington, Minn. "We have not taken a case to the courtroom since 1994," Byers added. About two-thirds of the claims were resolved by claims coordinators who have authority to settle claims after visiting with injured customers, according to Byers. The remaining third of the claims land in mediation and are settled before trial, he said. "It's just been a no-brainer," Byers said of the ADR program. "It's been wildly successful." The program has also led to cost savings for Toro. The average expense for handling a products liability claim has dropped from $115,000 in the early 1990s to $43,000, according to Byers. The average payout per claim fell from $68,368 in 1991 to $32,200 currently, he added.[78]

Workplace Disputes:

Perhaps more common than dispute management systems addressing commercial and product liability claims are those addressing workplace disputes. Such disputes are inevitable in any business with more than a handful of employees. Planning for and efficient management of such dispute can not only create substantial savings, but also improve morale and productivity.

---

[78] (Rooney, 2008).

In addition, such systems may be necessary to minimize and avoid significant liabilities associated with indifference to employee substantive rights. On one hand, implementation of a meaningful dispute resolution system can demonstrate management's good faith and reasonable care in avoiding misconduct by supervisors. In *Burlington Industries v. Ellerth*, 524 U.S. 724 (1998), the U.S. Supreme Court held that an employer can avoid liability for the misconduct of a supervisor if it can show (i) that the employer exercised "reasonable care" to prevent and promptly correct any sexual harassment, and (ii) that the employee unreasonably failed to take advantage of opportunities to correct or prevent the harm giving rise to the claim.

On the other hand, the absence of meaningful opportunities for redress can exacerbate liability risks. In *Faragher v. City of Boca Raton*, 524 U.S. 775 (1998), the Supreme Court held that where a supervisor has been given "unchecked authority" and employees are left "isolated from management," an employer may be held liable for the supervisor's creation of a hostile environment.

Of course, legal obligations that promote the development of workplace dispute resolutions systems may promote legally compliant but ineffective mechanisms. A company may be equally or more concerned about running afoul of *Faragher* than about effective dispute management. Assurances of an effective system can only be obtained by developing and testing meaningful measures of success, which may include measurements of cost savings, fewer disputes, and/or shorter disputes.[79]

CIGNA[80]

CIGNA has implemented a three-step process for resolving workplace disputes that includes two internal mechanisms to be followed, if necessary, by arbitration (and/or mediation if requested).

The first internal mechanism is called "Speak Easy" and addresses employment matters and encourages employees to discuss problems with local management and HR personnel. If local consultation is unsuccessful, the employee may confer with, and seek assistance from, an Employee Relations ("Speak Easy") consultant. If Phase II—consultation with the "Speak Easy Consultant"—is not successful, then the employee may seek arbitration in accordance with CIGNA's arbitration policy (which also allows for mediation if both parties consent).

---

[79] *See generally*, (Lipsky & Seeber, Emerging Systems for Managing Workplace Conflict, 2003); (CPR Institute for Dispute Resolution, 2002); (Slaikeu, 1998).

[80] CIGNA's program materials are included in (CPR Institute for Dispute Resolution, 2002).

CIGNA also offers an alternative "Peer Review" process to address issues related to the application and interpretation of company policies, procedures, and practices. Like Speak Easy, the Peer Review process is a two-step process that requires the employee first to discuss the matter locally before seeking appointment of a Peer Review Panel. Peer Review Panels are authorized to address policy matters, but they are not authorized to change established policies, pay levels or benefits, work schedules, employment decisions, or to grant monetary relief.

CIGNA Peer Review Panels comprise five members who have completed the required training and are drawn from three categories—supervisors, exempt employees who do not supervise, and nonexempt employees. Members are drawn from the different pools depending on whether the party with the grievance is a supervisor or nonsupervisor.

At the meeting of the Peer Review Panel, the employee can present his or her testimony and evidence and propose a remedy. Witnesses testify in confidence without others present. After consideration of the evidence, the Panel votes to grant, modify, or deny the proposed relief. The decision of the Panel is binding on CIGNA but not on the employee.

Employees may opt for either Speak Easy or Peer Review, but not both. If these measures are unsuccessful, the employee may seek arbitration/mediation.

CIGNA's arbitration rules impose significant limitations on the arbitration process. The rules provide that the Federal Arbitration Act will govern the arbitration and that the arbitrator must apply applicable statutory and case law. The rules further provide, however, that the arbitrator "will have no power to change CIGNA's policies… or to substitute his or her business judgment for that of CIGNA." In addition, the rules limit depositions to a total of two days and prohibit depositions of "any employee of CIGNA company who: (1) is not listed as a witness by CIGNA and (2) who certifies in writing to the arbitrator that he/she has no knowledge of the facts surrounding the dispute." Further, the party requesting the deposition is required to bear all of the related costs, including court reporter fees, transcript costs, and those related to office space.

CIGNA's rules further provide that the hearing will normally be completed in one day, unless the arbitrator decides that additional time is required for "good cause."

Finally, CIGNA rules provide that CIGNA will generally pay the full cost of the administrative fees for the arbitration (and the arbitrator's fees) in excess of the $100 to be paid by the employee. The rules provide for each party to bear its own legal fees and the expenses of their witnesses.

Halliburton

Halliburton has been a long-time proponent of workplace dispute resolution programs and has adopted a four-part program including an Open Door Policy, Internal Conference, Mediation, and finally Arbitration. In addition, Halliburton provides its employees with access to an ombudsman via a toll-free hotline and payment of up to $2,500 for legal consultation with counsel of its employee's choosing. Halliburton has stated that all but 2% of its workplace disputes are resolved without requiring arbitration.[81]

The Halliburton program covers all of its employees except those working outside the United States and the coverage of United States law. In addition, employees covered by a collective bargaining agreement are not covered. The program is mandatory for all employees and former employees (pursuant to their agreements with Halliburton).

Halliburton describes its open-door policy as providing the most immediate and preferred method for resolving disputes. The policy provides for access to supervisors, managers, and up through the managerial chain of responsibility. Halliburton's program materials state that "[a]lthough you are encouraged to solve your problem at the lowest possible level, you may take it as far up the chain of command as needed," and explain that this option is "encouraged because it's so easy to use, it promotes faster resolution than more formal options, and it reduces the risks of damaged relationships." Halliburton acknowledges that "most businesses prefer to resolve disputes this way—at the lowest possible level" and "we've just given it a formal name." Halliburton also emphasizes that retaliation is prohibited against any person initiating open-door discussions or any other dispute resolution process.

The Halliburton "Internal Conference Option" refers to a conference with a Halliburton ombudsman to discuss potential processes for resolving the issue. Those processes may include a return to open-door discussions, informal intervention by the ombudsman, internal mediation (with a trained employee mediator), external mediation or arbitration, or a custom process.

For mediation or arbitration, employees may contact the American Arbitration Association, the Judicial Arbitration Mediation Services (JAMS), or the CPR Institute for Dispute Resolution. The employee pays a $50 initiation fee but the remainder of the administrative charges are paid by Halliburton. Each party bears its own attorneys fees and witness costs (although the employee's legal fees may be covered by the Halliburton's legal consultation policy up to a specified level).

---

[81] (CPR Institute for Dispute Resolution, 2002, p. 43).

Halliburton specifies general rules for arbitration under its program. Those rules do not limit discovery, except to the extent that discovery restrictions are imposed by the arbitrator. The rules also provide that the arbitrator must follow applicable law and may not abridge or enlarge substantive rights.

Johnson & Johnson

Johnson & Johnson's dispute resolution program—called Common Ground—includes open door, facilitation (*i.e.,* meetings with a trained "facilitator"), and mediation. Unlike Halliburton's, Johnson & Johnson's program does not provide for arbitration in the event that the open door, its internal facilitation process, and mediation prove unsuccessful. Like Halliburton, however, Johnson & Johnson states that only 2% of its disputes fail to reach resolution during, or prior to, mediation.

U.S. Postal Service

Perhaps the most chronicled workplace dispute resolution program is the Redress* program of the U.S. Postal Service, which relies upon a form of mediation called "transformative" mediation. In contrast to "facilitative" mediation in which the mediator, through consultation with the parties and "shuttle" diplomacy, works to promote an agreed resolution to the dispute at hand, transformative mediation focuses on the relationship between the parties in dispute and assumes that the parties themselves are best able to decide whether and how to resolve their dispute. Transformative mediation focuses on empowering the parties to express themselves effectively and encourages them to recognize and respect each other's perspectives and motivations.

The USPS Redress program was, in fact, mandated in the settlement of a discrimination suit brought by African-American employees in Florida in the early 1990s. The goal of the program has been to not only promote cost-effective settlements of disputes, but to also improve the workplace environment (and reduce the likelihood of disputes).

The U.S. Postal Service Web site provides the following explanation of the differences between facilitative and transformative mediation:

How is Directive/Evaluative mediation different?

Many lawyers and representatives have experience with the "directive" or "evaluative" mediation model. Mediators with a directive orientation are trained to emphasize settlement and move parties toward that goal. They set guidelines for the parties' participation and may take a leading role in their discussions. They are solution-oriented and are actively involved in defining both the problem and its solution. They lead the process and draw the parties' attention away from emotion and towards solution of the immediate conflict. Long-term effects upon the parties' relationship are not an area of direct focus. They are trained to suggest possible outcomes and to evaluate the parties' relative positions. They often separate the parties into individual discussions (caucuses) in order to keep them moving in the direction the mediator believes has the best opportunity for reaching a settlement. The mediator declares success when both parties sign a settlement agreement.[82]

What does a transformative mediator do?

Transformative mediators operate from the belief that conflict presents opportunities for individuals to change (transform) their interactions with others. Parties can take advantage of these opportunities in mediation by exercising their abilities to make decisions and to gain perspective over their situations. The mediator support the parties as they decide what to discuss and set their own agenda. The mediator can be expected to summarize discussions, clarify issues, and promote confidence in making decisions. The mediator can achieve this by "reflecting", "summarizing", "checking in" and by asking "open ended questions" only. Anything outside of that scope does not fit into the transformative framework. The mediation is considered successful when the parties have a clearer understanding of their situation and better recognize each other's perspective and have interactive communication. Often, this leads to resolution of the dispute.

What will a transformative mediator refrain from doing?

Transformative mediators will not direct the content of the mediation, will not "gather" information for settlement purposes or take an active role in the decision-making process. Instead, they support the parties with the process. They will not push the parties towards settlement, even if they

---

[82] The USPS description of traditional mediation is, unfortunately, an oversimplification. A sophisticated mediator will always help the parties gain a better understanding of their own and opposing parties' interests in attempting to encourage a settlement in both parties' interests. Because all mediation depends on the parties' agreement for success, the notion that a mediator can simply tell the parties how the case should settle and expect them to agree to his or her views is both naïve and contrary to effective practice. Further, and as described in Chapter II, the notion that the parties themselves will know what is fair and how best to settle their dispute, without the insights of a neutral third party that may help them overcome potentially harmful psychological biases, may also be unrealistic.

believe they "know" how the case can fairly settle. "Forced" settlements do not resolve the underlying conflict. They will not suggest whether one party's viewpoint has more merit than the other's. They will not comment on the strength or weakness of either party's case or on the status of the law or company policy.

Transformative mediators will not discourage the parties from exhibiting their emotions. Seeing the other party's emotional response may allow parties to better understand the impact of their words and actions.[83]

Although it has not reported financial savings as a result of its program, the USPS has reported both a relatively high success rate (77%) in resolving disputes and high employee satisfaction with the program.

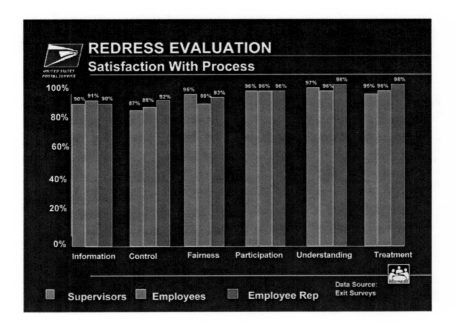

---

[83] Available at http://www.usps.com/redress/a_trans.htm.

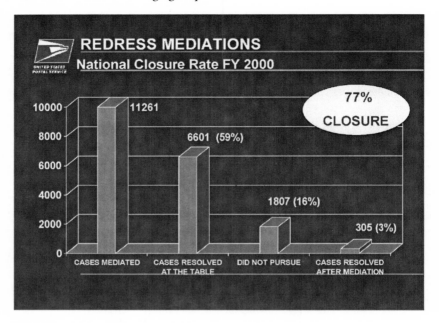

Medical Dispute Systems

Medical malpractice claims have accounted for perhaps the most vocal criticism of traditional litigation. Malpractice litigation has led to countless calls for tort law reform and has often been blamed for driving physicians from practice in high-risk fields, such as obstetrics and gynecology, because of the resulting high costs of insurance.

Recent case studies of dispute management by certain progressive hospitals, however, suggest that malpractice litigation (and its extraordinary costs) can be dramatically reduced through dispute management systems that include apologies and expressions of concern to affected patients and their families. Just as The Toro Company has dramatically reduced product liability litigation by treating injured customers with respect and offering a prompt avenue for addressing their concerns, health care systems have been able to dramatically reduce malpractice claims by like measures.

University of Pittsburgh Medical Center

The University of Pittsburgh Medical Center, the largest health system and employer in Western Pennsylvania, has achieved stunning success within the first three years of its program to address healthcare-related disputes with prompt intervention and mediation. UPMC's program is designed to reduce uncertainty and lower costs, while promoting patient safety.

Since inception of its program in October 2004 through January 2008, UPMC resolved 90% of the 117 cases that entered its mediation program in advance of trial. Of those cases, 101 either settled during mediation or shortly thereafter. Further, as explained by UPMC counsel Richard P. Kidwell and Robert Voinchet, the settlement rate was reflected in substantial reductions of legal expense. [84]

> In February 2005, after the first few months of the mediation program, the expenses incurred in mediated cases were compared against those in cases that were tried to plaintiffs' verdicts or were settled in the same dollar range as the mediated cases. Mediation expenses averaged approximately $75,000 less per case than the expenses in cases tried or settled. When this same analysis was done in February 2006, the savings averaged about $65,000 less per mediated case. This slight decrease is attributable to increased efficiency in overseeing litigated cases. Another analysis compared the timing of the mediation process in two sets of mediated cases. The first set consisted of cases that were reported prior to the initiation of the UPMC mediation program but were resolved at mediation. The second set consisted of cases that were reported after initiation of the UPMC mediation program and were settled at mediation. The average length of time between opening and closing the files in the first set was 1,126 days and the defense costs averaged slightly in excess of 569,000. Those same averages in the second set of cases were 276 days and just under 523,000.[85]

The success of UPMC program, moreover, demonstrates the significant savings and related benefit that can be realized with only modest changes to a health care organization's processes and orientation. UPMC's dispute management program rests on four main elements: (1) inclusion of a mediation agreement in the documents to be executed by patients upon intake; (2) identification of mediators available to address disputes in a timely manner; (3) educational materials about the program for patients; (4) an easy mechanism for patients and their families to enter into mediation.

Based on a similar mediation agreement used by John Hopkins University Hospital, UPMC requests patients to execute the following:

---

[84] (Kidwell & Voinchet).
[85] Ibid.

AGREEMENT TO MEDIATE CLAIMS

By initialing below, I agree that any claim which may result from the care provided to me by the doctors, nurses and other healthcare providers in any UPMC facility shall be subject to the laws of Pennsylvania. I also agree that before any lawsuit is filed related to the care provided to me, I must attempt to resolve any claim through mediation, which must take place in the Commonwealth of Pennsylvania. I am not waiving my right to a jury trial. Mediation is a process in which a neutral third person tries to help settle a claim. This agreement is binding on me and any person making a claim on my behalf.

In contrast to John Hopkins' program, UPMC's program is not mandatory and it is not a condition for treatment. Despite permitting patients to opt out of the program, UPMC has achieved nearly the same settlement rate as John Hopkins.[86]

In addition to its mediation program for malpractice claims, UPMC has implemented a separate mediation program to address general concerns about patient services. UPMC calls this second program "intermediation," which it describes in patient education materials, as follows:

What is intermediation?
Intermediation is a new option to resolve concerns or issues at UPMC. There is no direct cost to you. It is a dialogue between you and your health care providers. The discussion is led by a neutral third party called a mediator. It is an opportunity for you and your health care providers to sit down for a face-to-face meeting, respond to each other, and resolve concerns that you may have about care or services.

Who picks the neutral mediator to lead the face-to-face meeting?
Patients or their family members who request intermediation have the option to select a neutral, third-party mediator. UPMC has identified nine mediators from a variety of different backgrounds for the intermediation program. Their photos and brief biographies are provided in this brochure.

---

[86] (Kidwell and Voinchet).

Who pays for the services of the mediator?

There is no cost to you. Neutral mediators are paid on a case-by-case basis and for their expenses by UPMC. However, the mediators are not UPMC employees and are paid only for the services they provide.

University of Michigan Health System

The New York Times recently reported on a similarly successful dispute management system used by the University of Michigan Medical Center:

> For decades, malpractice lawyers and insurers have counseled doctors and hospitals to "deny and defend." Many still warn clients that any admission of fault, or even expression of regret, is likely to invite litigation and imperil careers.
>
> But with providers choking on malpractice costs and consumers demanding action against medical errors, a handful of prominent academic medical centers, like Johns Hopkins and Stanford, are trying a disarming approach.
>
> By promptly disclosing medical errors and offering earnest apologies and fair compensation, they hope to restore integrity to dealings with patients, make it easier to learn from mistakes and dilute anger that often fuels lawsuits.
>
> * * *
>
> At the University of Michigan Health System ["UMHS"], one of the first to experiment with full disclosure, existing claims and lawsuits dropped to 83 in August 2007 from 262 in August 2001.[87]

It has also been reported that, after implementing its program, UMHS's defense litigation costs decreased from an average of $65,000 per case to $35,000 per case for a cumulative savings of $2 million annually. Consequently, UMHS's annual attorney fees have dropped from $3 million in 2002 to $1 million in 2005.[88]

Veterans' Administration Hospital and Rush Medical Center

Among the first heath care institution to adopt a proactive approach to dispute resolution was the Veterans' Administration Hospital in Lexington, Kentucky. The hospital has a policy to share with patients and their families any medical error or mistake and, in fact, to inform them of their right to seek relief. The

---

[87] (Sack, 2008).

[88] (Atwood, 2008).

policy has been remarkably successful. In the 17 years since the Lexington Hospital adopted its policy of communicating medical errors, it has an average claim payout of $16,000. By contrast, the national average settlement for a medical malpractice case by a VA Hospital is $98,000.[89]

A somewhat different, but also effective, program was initiated by Chicago's Rush Medical Center in 1995 to respond to increasing legal costs. Rush Medical Center uses a mediation agreement that provides for an exchange of submissions and brief presentations by each side at a mediation conference, which is then followed by discussions in caucus with each side. The unique feature of the program is that it provides for co-mediation (*i.e.,* mediation with two mediators), with each side selecting one of the mediators. The mediators are chosen respectively from lists of trained plaintiffs and defense malpractice attorneys. In the first five years of the program (1995–2000), 80% of the 55 malpractice cases submitted for mediation were resolved in much less time than comparable nonmediated cases in the area.

Further, the settlement payments were generally less than in nonmediated cases. Although Rush Medical Center was concerned that the relatively quick and cost-effective co-mediation program might increase claims, there was actually as slight reduction in the number of lawsuits filed during this time.[90]

Case Study Conclusions

As shown by the foregoing examples, dispute management systems or programs have proven extraordinarily successful across the broad range of commonplace disputes affecting modern businesses, including those arising from the workplace, commercial relationships, consumer transactions, and heath care services. Given this track record, more remarkable than the successes of sundry dispute management programs is the fact that such programs are not more widespread.

Further, even businesses that have successfully implemented programs to address disputes in one area, such as workplace disputes, may fail to do so in other areas, such as commercial or healthcare disputes. Thus, Georgia Pacific, while achieving great savings from its program to manage commercial disputes, has not apparently implemented a program to address internal workplace disputes. Healthcare systems may adopt dispute resolution programs for malpractice claims but not for workplace or commercial disputes, and so on.

---

[89] Ibid.

[90] *See* (Cooley, 2002) and (Guadagnino, 2004). UPMC and Johns Hopkins have similarly found that mediation programs have reduced their malpractice lawsuits. Telephone conversation with R. Kidwell, November 14, 2008.

Such circumstances suggest the presence of significant impediments to the development of seemingly necessary programs to address entirely predictable disputes in a rational manner.

CHAPTER X: Development and Implementation of Dispute Management Systems

The design of a successful dispute resolution program calls for the same systematic diligence needed to implement any significant change affecting a corporation's culture, infrastructure, and key policies. Senior management must support the initiative and provide the necessary resources for design and implementation. Perhaps even more importantly, the likely parties to disputes to be included in the system must be educated about, and persuaded to use, a new ADR process rather than persist in entrenched but inefficient prior procedures.

If the organizational and psychological impediments to ADR can be overcome, an efficient program can be designed and implemented with well-established protocols for system development applicable across a broad range of disciplines.

Impediments to the Adoption of ADR

Although the impediments to development of dispute resolution programs have not been as rigorously studied as such programs themselves, the same factors that promote the persistence of irrational litigation may be at least partly to blame. For example, unrealistic optimism about the prospects for costly litigation may induce complacency. Similarly, a company may have unrealistic views about its ability to control or manage litigation costs and outcomes.

In addition, a company may believe that proactive engagement, communication, and especially apologies may be considered signs of weakness that will encourage groundless or weak claims to be initiated. A USA Today story about corporate apologies reported that "Lawyers representing the company often discourage it [an apology] for fear of lawsuits from consumers."[91] And some commentators have argued that our legal system discourages apologies on the theory that "what you say can, and will, be held against you."[92] On the other hand, studies suggest that the most important factor leading to medical

---

[91] (Adams, 2000)
[92] *See, e.g.,* (Tyler, 1997).

malpractice lawsuits is ineffective (or nonexistent) communications with injured patients and their families.[93]

In perhaps the most comprehensive study of corporate strategies for addressing workplace disputes, the authors explained that "the choice of an organization's conflict management strategy [or lack of strategy] we discovered, often reflects the [key] decision makers' dominant disposition regarding the nature of conflict."[94] Some companies opt to fight every battle to the hilt, premised on views that conflict implies pure winners and pure losers and, further, that aggressive responses to conflict are needed to discourage future claims. Other companies recognize the diverse range of disputes and that disputes often admit a range of possible resolutions—many of which may be beneficial to both sides.

In addition, dispositions toward ADR and its potential savings may also reflect the economic and market condition of the subject company. A highly profitable and/or monopolistic company may have little concern about the potential savings from ADR and prefer to maintain an image of aggressiveness in responding to opponents—in all spheres. Further, such a company may simply assume that it is likely to have deeper pockets than its opponents and, therefore, can more readily take advantage of the ability to impose costs on its opposition through litigation. On the other hand, cost-sensitive and/or competitive businesses may have a greater need to manage disputes to protect their bottom lines.

Reluctance to initiate a dispute management program and/or ADR generally may also stem from internal company political motivations or "agency" problems. Although the companies' long-term interests might benefit from ADR, managers with responsibility for disputes may have an interest in preserving the status quo and using "tried and true" methods rather than taking a risk on new processes. Managers may erroneously perceive that they have greater control over litigation than ADR or may prefer the safety of being able to blame the lawyers for problems that may arise in litigation or for budget-busting expenses.

Lack of knowledge—both about the inefficiency and uncertainty of litigation and about the benefits of alternatives — also accounts for the slow

---

[93] (Leibman & Hyman, 2004). Approximately 30 states have responded to this impediment to dispute resolution by adopting laws to prevent the use of apologies as an admission of guilt or liability. *See, e.g.,* California Evidence Code Section 1160 (2001). Most of the "apology" laws provide immunity for "expressions of sympathy" and the like, but not admissions of fault. This tenuous distinction may, to a significant extent, undermine the effectiveness of such laws in promoting frank communication at the outset of a dispute.

[94] (Lipsky & Seeber, Emerging Systems for Managing Workplace Conflict, 2003, p. 119).

adoption of efficient ADR processes. Thus, businesses most likely to agree to ADR in advance of a dispute are those with the most ADR experience.[95] On the other hand, lack of experience with ADR is often cited as a reason for refusing to pursue ADR. [96]

Finally, perhaps the most significant impediment to adoption of efficient ADR and dispute management systems is good, old fashioned, inertia. History is replete with examples of good (and even essential) ideas that were ignored or ridiculed for challenging the status quo.[97]

Healthcare and hygiene provides the most notable examples of the inability of good ideas to spread of their own accord. For example, scurvy was the bane of sailors for centuries. When Vasco de Gama successfully circled the Cape of Good Hope in 1498-9, over half of his crew of 160 died from scurvy during the voyage. In 1601, a British sea captain named John Lancaster discovered that he could completely prevent scurvy by giving sailors a little lime juice every day. This cure, however, was not fully adopted by the British Navy until 1865. [98]

Similarly, by the late 1840s, Dr. Ignaz Semmelweis had demonstrated the unequivocal effectiveness and importance of handwashing for avoiding infections in clinical settings. His efforts to encourage handwashing, and those of other early handwashing proponents like Dr. Oliver Wendell Holmes, were rejected for decades, until well after his death from infection in 1865. [99]

Successful Dispute Management and Paradigm Change

Professors David Lipsky, Ronald Seeber, and Richard Fincher posit that an "internal champion" is essential to development of a dispute management system for the workplace. Although their discussion focuses on programs to address workplace disputes, their reasoning applies across the range of common disputes:

> The majority of workplace system efforts have one internal champion, typically a senior executive. If a crisis initiated the effort [to develop a dispute management program], the champion is often the leader in whose function the crisis occurred. If there was no precipitating crises, the champion is not necessarily the original visionary, however. It could be the general counsel, or even the quality control executive.

---

[95] (Lipsky & Seeber, In search for control: The Corporate Embrace of ADR, 1998).
[96] (Lipsky & Seeber, Emerging Systems for Managing Workplace Conflict, 2003, p. 110).
[97] (Rogers, 2003)
[98] (Berwick, 2003).
[99] (Larson, 1989).

The internal champion is important because he or she will lead the effort to embellish the business case and start socializing the proposal to the executive team. Aligning the process with an internal champion is important because in many cases this individual plays a continuing role in the implementation process, including ensuring financial support. The champion requires education as to the scope of the effort and anticipates obstacles in the organization. The champion is rarely a subject matter expert on workplace systems; rather his or her passion often derives from solid business intuition. The first key role for the internal champion is to focus on the business case and gain its acceptance by the senior leadership.[100]

This imperative for an internal champion or one or more "influence leaders,"[101] however, may be but part of an effective strategy to motivate an organization to adopt a new and better process. Most significantly, research demonstrates that it is not enough for a business or nonprofit to explain a good (or even great) idea to its workforce, customers, patients, suppliers or partners and wait for it to be understood and adopted. Instead, changing a longstanding practice (however wasteful or damaging) requires identification of two or three critical behaviors that serve as triggers for the targeted practice and the use of multiple influence strategies to encourage those behaviors.[102]

Critical or vital behaviors often act like one-way gateways to either entrenched but misguided pathways or innovative, better, ones. When you return your rental car and cross the one-way spikes in the driveway, even though it is simply to late to fill up the tank and thereby avoid the penalty for returning a less than full tank.

Human interactions and processes key behaviors work much the same way: if you can identify the behaviors that serve as gateways to paths that avoid waste and promote productivity, and persuade people to adopt those behaviors, the preferred paths become seemingly unavoidable and inevitable.

Why are multiple strategies needed to promote beneficial and seemingly simple changes? In simplest terms, because people are not computers with on/off switches, but comprise multiple and often competing human traits affecting both motives and resulting behaviors. Often it is not enough to win over someone's

---

[100] (Lipsey, Fincher & Seeger, 2003).

[101] In his seminal work, "Diffusion of Innovations," Professor Everett M. Rogers explains the critical role played by "opinion leaders" in leading adoption of innovative ideas. Everett's work implies that it may not enough to have an "internal champion promote a new dispute systems in an organization. Instead, change must be supported by "opinion leaders" among the likely participants in a new system. (Rogers, 2003).

[102] (Patterson, Grenny, Maxfield, McMillan, & Switzer, 2008).

mind to a new idea, but you must also win over his or her heart and instincts. For dispute resolution systems, the focus of such education and persuasion will be the parties and potential parties to disputes leading to wasteful and often unnecessary litigation such as suppliers, customers, employees and patients.

In *The Happiness Hypothesis*,[103] Psychology Professor Jonathan Haidt uses the metaphor of a person riding an elephant to explain why it can be so difficult to stop even destructive behaviors that we fully understand to be harmful (like smoking, overeating, etc.). The person (*i.e.*, the rider) represents the rational, most modern (in an evolutionary sense) part of the brain, while the elephant represents the more primitive emotional and instinctive.

> Modern theories of rational choice and information processing don't adequately explain weakness of the will. Older metaphors about controlling animals work beautifully.... The image that I came up with for myself as I marveled at my weaknesses, was that I was a rider on the back of elephant. I'm holding the reins in my hands, and by pulling one way or the other I can tell the elephant to turn, stop, or go. I can direct things but only when the elephant doesn't have desires of his own. When the elephant wants to do something, I'm no match for him.
>
> ... To understand the most important ideas in psychology, you need to understand however the mind is divided into arts that some times conflict. We assume that there is one person in each body, but in some ways we are each more like a committee whose members have been thrown together to do a job but who often find themselves working at cross purposes.[104]

Multiple influence strategies, therefore, are often essential to persuade even well informed groups of diverse individuals to adopt even seemingly benign but beneficial new behaviors and processes.

With respect to dispute management, some improvements can be accomplished simply by compelling disputants to make use of ADR. In an increasing number of courts and companies, disputants are required at least to try mediation or other form of ADR as a predicate to, or substitute for, litigation. On the other hand, there can be no doubt that the most effective use of ADR, and greatest savings, can be achieved only with the willing (if not enthusiastic) participation of the parties. Indeed, every successful ADR program described in the prior chapter makes use of one or more strategy to change minds and behaviors while proving the necessary infrastructure for managing disputes.

---

[103] (Haidt, 2006).

[104] (Haidt, 2006, p. 4-5).

A recent work discussing successful "influence strategies" for organizations and societies describes six strategies that can help align rational, emotional, and instinctive sentiments in favor of beneficial change.[105] Those influence strategies include (1) providing positive and negative personal incentives to encourage the critical behaviors that precipitate change; (2) training to facilitate use of, and comfort with, the new process; (3) providing direct personal and vicarious experiences with the new process to overcome distrust and risk aversion; (4) providing mechanisms for social support (and peer pressure) to encourage the desired behaviors; (5) providing tools for, and easy access to, new methods; and (6) creating organization or program structures that align with, rather than impede, the desired changes. While successful implementation of a new program that changes long-standing practice may not require deployment of every potential influence strategy, reliance on a single strategy alone is unlikely to succeed.

With respect to implementation of a dispute management system, the range and extent of strategies needed to win over the nature of the likely disputes, other factors affecting the circumstances of predictable disputes. In contrast to attempts to alter pleasurable bad habits, like overeating, smoking, drinking, etc., efforts to promote ADR have the benefit of addressing a subject of near universal dissatisfaction: few people relish the idea of spending years in costly legal battles to achieve an uncertain result in court

Dispute management systems have a second advantage relative to other programs directed at productive system changes. The two vital behaviors necessary for productive change are easy to identify.

The first vital behavior for efficient dispute resolution is simply to expect and plan for disputes. Although in some cases, significant savings and efficiencies can be achieved by deploying ADR after a dispute arises, in many (if not most) cases, the initiation of a dispute so taints and distorts the landscape and parties' motives that meaningful managerial controls are implausible. Again, while this vital behavior seems obvious, it is hardly commonplace. As noted in Chapter II, all of us have an ingrained tendency to underestimate the likelihood that bad things will happen to us (or our organizations) and this human basis exhibits its full force with respect to the prospects for costly and time-consuming litigation.

The second vital behavior for an effective dispute management system is to get parties to ADR to overcome natural distrust and deploy ADR when a dispute arises, rather than after it has festered and grown into a morass. This key behavior may not always be necessary to put a dispute management system in

---

[105] (Patterson, Grenny, Maxfield, McMillan, & Switzer, 2008).

place, but it is invariably essential for the system to work well. This key behavior is most frequently, and sensibly, addressed by providing education and/or training related to the system and by making it both easy to access and to use.

In planning for predictable disputes, business and nonprofit organization face disputes that fall into two main categories: (i) external disputes with independent parties and organizations, and (ii) internal workplace disputes. Although there is significant overlap—for example, a badly managed work place dispute can transform itself into a class action by disgruntled (and now independent) ex-employees—the two types of dispute require different managerial solutions.

External and internal disputes differ not primarily because they tend to concern different subjects (*e.g.*, breach of contract or medical error for external disputes, and discrimination and other employment law claims for internal disputes), but because the relationships affected by internal and external disputes are typically governed by distinct legal, organizational, and social norms and interests.

Broadly classifying disputes into two simple categories is undeniably an over simplification. Not only will disputes in each category arise in innumerable circumstance, but also dispute management must consider the implications of the likely parties' respective bargaining power and the time horizons affecting such power. For example, a company (or individual) may have far more power to affect the management of disputes before entering business relationship than after the relationship has begun. As discussed below, such distinctions and issues should be addressed when designing a dispute management system to address particular needs of an organization and the predictable disputes it is likely to confront. For purposes of approaching dispute management in a systematic and efficient manner, however, external and internal disputes suggest distinct frameworks.

Dispute Management Systems for Healthcare and Business Relationship

In many respects, it is far easier to design and implement a dispute management system for external relationships, such those related to purchases and supply or physicians and patients, than to address internal disputes. Most importantly, external relationships typically center on a discrete subject (such as medical care or technology supply) and provide a single access point or, at least, focal point for defining the terms of the overall relationship (including the potential for disputes).

Healthcare provides the most straight-forward example. Once providers are persuaded to plan for potential disputes, a system can be implemented (as shown by UPMC and others) by, for example, including a mediation agreement in patient documents. Today, patients already expect to sign a variety of consent forms, privacy agreement, assurances of payment and other forms in advance of treatment. The addition of a mediation agreement is likely to seem sensible to patients—assuming it is even noticed. As shown by the Air Force and Georgia Pacific ADR programs, agreements to mediate or use other ADR mechanisms are similarly non-controversial in many commercial settings.

As noted above, entry of agreement to mediate or arbitrate alone is insufficient to realize the full potential of a dispute management system for external disputes. The agreement could be ignored until the problem giving rise to the dispute has become intractable, or the ADR agreement itself could become the subject of litigation.

Instead, a dispute management system for external disputes should provide education and encouragement to use the system to address disputes promptly. In healthcare, for example, malpractice suits are often filed not because of an unintended medical mistake but because of poor communication with patients and families who are left to assume the worst. A dispute system that provides for mediation, but which does not respond quickly to this underlying cause of many costly claims, may have little benefit and may even make matters worse by heightening, rather than reducing, cynicism as to the provider's motives and concern.

To encourage effective use, an ADR system must invariably be easy to access and use. The more difficult as system is to use, and the more costly for intended participants, the more likely they are to revert to the status quos of non-communication and traditional litigation.

Dispute Management Systems for the Workplace

Workplace dispute management systems may be more costly to implement than systems for external dispute, but have the potential to foster even greater rewards. Workplace system must be designed to address an organization's unique, and invariably complex, preexisting network of internal relationships.

In contrast to systems addressing external disputes, which typically have an obvious focus, a system addressing internal dispute has the potential for addressing a range of subjects. The starting point for such a system, therefore, is reaching a decision as to such basic questions as the types of disputes that will be covered and for whom. Specifically:

(1)   Who will be included—active employees, retirees, terminated employees, independent contractors? Will union matters be addressed through ADR?

(2)   What types of disputes will be covered or excluded? Sometimes identifying the scope of a system by articulating the types of disputes that are excluded is easier. For example, it may be necessary to exclude contract disputes, disputes covered by specific laws or regulations, and/or crimes or serious policy violations (such as drug use).

(3)   Will participation be mandatory or voluntary? In either case, participation must be documented by written agreements.

(4)   What steps are needed to trigger participation? Given the universal goal of early intervention to keep small disputes small, mechanisms for raising issues and entering the resolution system should be both simple and nonthreatening.

(5)   What dispute resolution mechanisms will be used? Common mechanisms include both internal mechanisms, such as "open-door policies," ombudsmen, hot lines, managerial conferences, peer mediation, facilitators, and, if necessary, external mechanism including third party mediation and arbitration.

(6)   How will costs be covered?

(7)   How will unresolved disputes be handled?

(8)   What safeguards will be employed to assure fairness and how will participation be promoted?[106]

After addressing these questions, an efficient system can be developed through five main phases that track well-established protocols for designing and developing products or information systems. First, the system's requirements must be identified and crafted into a "high-level" design setting forth key objectives and identifying the system's overall scope. Second, those requirements must be transformed into an architecture or blueprint providing an overall framework for the system and explaining how its various elements will interact with each other. Third, based on the requirements and architecture, the components of the system—in the case of ADR program, the program documents and materials—must be crafted and an infrastructure developed. Fourth, the program should be tested, checked for deficiencies, and refined. Finally, after implementation, the program should be monitored, evaluated, and refined as necessary to achieve its desired objectives. Each of these phases is discussed more fully below.

---

[106] *See generally*, (Lipsky, Seeber & Fincher, 2003); (CPR Institute for Dispute Resolution, 2002); (Slaikeu, 1998).

System Design Phase I: Project Requirements and Scope

The starting point for establishing a dispute resolution program or system is, of course, to develop the "business case" and/or overview of the project describing its anticipated components, scope, and goals. Unfortunately, this may not be as easy as it sounds, especially if an organization lacks experience with ADR and/or includes within its culture and management some of the impediments to the ADR discussed above.

To a great extent, the initial phase of project design will require the collection and assessment of both internal information and data related to historical and, therefore, predictable areas of repetitive disputes and, to the extent possible, benchmarking based upon the experience of similarly situated business. Analysis of such data will help identify key areas of potential savings and facilitated preparation of the business case needed to elicit managerial commitment and support.

As part of this assessment, it may be helpful (if not essential) to conduct focus groups and/or other meetings with potential stakeholders—especially with respect to plans for workplace disputes. Among other benefits, early involvement in the design of a dispute management system may help overcome potential cynicism or even hostility to implementation of the final program.

The business case (and project overview) must also consider such issues as organizational structure, corporate culture, the presence or absence of collective bargaining relationships, and internal experience with, and attitudes towards, ADR. In addition, any legal restrictions, such as collective bargaining agreements, must be considered. Each of these factors may influence decisions as to the range of disputes to be included in the program, identification of eligible (or required) participants, anticipated education and training requirements, and dispute resolution alternations. In some instances, existing corporate structures can be modified or improved for the program, while in others it may be necessary to establish new structures entirely.

Depending on the nature of the business and its internal capabilities, initial planning should consider whether to develop the program only with in-house resources or to retain outside assistance. In either case, given the inherent relationships between a dispute resolution program, corporate culture, and, potentially, corporate morale, a strong internal presence on the design team is essential.

The end result of the first phase of project design may take the form of a Request for Proposal (RFP), or internal contract or commitment document. The RFP or commitment document should identify expectations, roles and responsibilities, costs, and deliverables to be associated with each subsequent

Development Process For Dispute Management Systems

phase of the design project. Like any significant corporate undertaking, both the design and implementation of a dispute resolution should be accompanied by clear benchmarks, measures of accountability, and testable results.

System Design Phase II: Project Architecture

Although the essential parameters of a dispute resolution system may be identified when defining project requirements, the framework for an effective system will likely require additional refinement once a commitment has been made to pursue development. In addition to the design of the dispute resolution mechanisms, it is commonly necessary to develop capabilities for training and education, internal marketing, personnel and infrastructure resources and responsibilities, program monitoring and assessment, and legal review.

In addition, during the architecture phase of design, the interactions between the various components of the programs should be defined and mapped out. In essence, a flow chart, blueprint, or system diagram should be created that allows for subsequent creation and build out of the various elements of the system to complement each other and foster achievement of the programs objectives.

For example, one of the most import design elements commonly included in effective dispute resolution systems are mechanisms that encourage early identification and resolution of disputes (and potential disputes) through collaboration and/or facilitated discussions (with ombuds or internal mediators) at the organizational levels closest to the origin of the problem. Addressing problems quickly and proactively can do much to keep small problems small and prevent them from growing into costly and time-consuming disputes.

As noted above, Halliburton encourages its employees to pursue "Open Door" resolution, because "it promotes faster [and less expensive] resolution than more formal options, and it reduces the risks of damaged relationships." The necessary corollary of an open door policy or other efforts to encourage direct or even facilitated negotiation are assurances against retaliation or other harmful consequences of a good faith effort to resolve concerns. Depending upon an organization's culture and history, assurances sufficient to overcoming cynicism and fears about the consequences of voicing concern may require far more than mere posting of a "no retaliation" policy or even internal marketing—it may require the development of trust and goodwill through good faith operation of the program itself.

The architecture should also consider the extent to which the system will rely on internal or external dispute resolution options and the interplay among them. As shown above, many successful systems seek to encourage internal/

direct lines of communication and collaboration as a predicate to more costly external measures, such as third party mediation, arbitration, and/or judicial resolution.

In the context of workplace disputes, preliminary internal measures commonly include open door policies, peer review, and/or facilitated discussion. In commercial relationships, a ladder of negotiations may be required—for example, project managers followed by division heads—in advance of mediation, arbitration, and/or litigation.

Assuming external/third-party neutrals (mediators, "early neutral evaluators," or arbitrators) will be called upon for matters not resolved through early intervention and preliminary internal measure, relationships with dispute resolution organizations with rosters of qualified neutrals (such as the American Arbitration Association, CPR Institute, National Arbitration Association, American Health Lawyers Association, etc.) should be considered.

System Design Phase III: Build Out

Based upon the completed architecture, the necessary policies, agreements, resources, and personnel can be put into place.

First, an effective dispute resolution system is likely to require ongoing oversight and support, including budgetary resources and dedicated personnel. Lipsky, Seeber, and Fincher explain that "[e]xperience has demonstrated that dedicated resources must be allocated to a person or function to manage the system and monitor its effectiveness."[107] Oversight of the system may be assigned to ombuds, a system coordinator, sourcing personnel, the legal department, or human resources personnel depending upon the nature and scope of the intended system.

Second, company governance and operations documents must be created. These documents include policy statements, contracts and contract clauses (workplace, commercial, and/or consumer agreements), employee manuals, training and educational materials, and forms to allow for operation of the system itself. Such documents may be created in paper or electronic form, depending on the capabilities and culture of the business.

Third, mechanisms for evaluating the system must be created. Such mechanisms may include statistical frameworks, surveys, and/or questionnaires that provide a basis for comparing system efficiency (in terms of both performance and savings) with appropriate benchmarks—either past dispute resolution experiences with comparable matters or comparable matters that fall outside the system.

---

[107] (Lipsky, Seeber & Fincher, 2003, p. 245).

In addition, consideration should be given to the collateral benefits (or harms) of a system. For example, how will the system affect employee morale and/or productivity, employee turnover, goodwill among customer, contractors, and/or suppliers, etc.? In discussing the benefits of The Toro Company's dispute resolution system, for example, Toro cited not only improved insurance relationships and ratings, but also positive publicity including an article in a business journal that described a mother who sued Toro after her son was killed in an accident involving a Toro product, but who "now has only good things to say about the company."[108]

System Design Phase IV: Testing, Refinement, and Implementation

If possible, a new dispute resolution system should be tested and refined. Two testing methods are plausible. Most commonly, dispute resolution systems are tested through pilot projects involving real problems and real disputes. The pilot can be rolled out at one company location, in one division, or with respect to a limited set of disputes.

Alternatively, a dispute resolution system can be tested in much the same way as many complex information technology systems can be, with hypothetical data and test scripts. Such testing of a dispute resolution system can be accomplished in conjunction with, and can promote, education, training, and internal marketing of the system. In the training of arbitrators and mediators, there is now a long history of using role-play scripts based upon hypothetical disputes.

Use of either or both test methods allows for refinement of system elements, preliminary assessment of performance, and the incremental incorporation of a new system into a company's culture.

Once the company has obtained some comfort and experience with its new dispute resolution method, full-scale implementation will have the greatest prospect for proceeding smoothly and effectively.

System Design Phase V: Monitoring, Assessment, and Improvement

Once the system is in place, monitoring and assessment allow for continued improvement. Common benchmarks for evaluating the financial benefits of a system include measures of case disposition, such as duration, cost (including both payouts and costs of the disputes themselves), and resolution rates. In addition to financial assessments, companies often assess program quality through surveys, questions, and commentaries from participants.

---

[108] (Trevarthen).

Modern business commonly focuses on "managing for results," which requires objective measures of progress and success.[109] Given the extraordinary savings and benefits achievable from prevention and efficient management of disputes (and avoidance of litigation), monitoring and measuring the success (or short comings) of a dispute resolution system is a sensible adjunct to system development and implementation.

---

[109] The Maxwell School of the Syracuse University offers a useful summary of ADR's place in an organization's strategic planning and the importance of measuring progress toward strategic objective in a Web site entitled "Performance Measurement for ADR Professionals," available at http://sites.maxwell.syr.edu/measuringADR/default.asp. (The Maxwell School, Syracuse University).

CHAPTER XI: *The Future: Online Dispute Resolution and Virtual Sessions*

Over the past 15 years, information technology has dramatically altered the landscape of modern business by improving communications, productivity, and means of collaboration. In the courtroom, litigation often becomes a spectacle of video presentations, simulations, and demonstrations that hold jurors in rapt attention, as if watching an episode of the latest television legal drama.

In some respects, ADR is not suited to the dazzle of modern technology. At its core, ADR focuses on repairing or redressing broken relationships. Effective mediation requires the cultivation of trust built upon empathy, understanding, and informed reasoning. Efficient arbitration may require assessment of personal credibility. Without a doubt, the optimal setting for ADR involves in-person interaction among respectful and committed participants. But if a key promise of ADR is cost-efficient management of disputes, then as with respect to other aspects of modern business (and society), the ability of information to reduce costs has, and will continue, to shape its future.

Meanwhile, technology—in particular the Internet and ecommerce—has expanded the nature and scope of business relationships and, accordingly, potential disputes. Most significantly, commerce and communications are no longer geographically constrained. Anyone with a computer anywhere in the world can trade with anyone else. Ecommerce is global commerce. Voice over IP (VoIP) services allow for literally costless communications, meetings, conferences, and collaboration with global participants.

Unfortunately, global commerce invariably precipitates global disputes. Further, because the Internet increases the scope and breadth of anonymous transactions—where the buyers and sellers have no prior relationship and lack other traditional means of developing trust—disputes may be especially likely. Likewise, the sheer speed and ease of technology-assisted transactions may further promote disputes by preventing reliance on practical but "nonlegal" safeguards to limit unauthorized uses of information. For example, court records have always been "public" information. Prior to the Internet, however, the administrative difficulty of obtaining those records largely protected them from undisciplined dissemination. Electronic filing and the Internet have eliminated this practical safeguard. Similarly, the Internet has largely eliminated any practical constraints on the dissemination of false or defamatory information.

In addition, the new relationships, products, services, and forms of intellectual property (such as domain names) have themselves created new subject matter for disputes.

While the nature and scope of commercial disputes have expanded along with the Internet and other forms of information technology, mechanisms for resolving those disputes have struggled to keep pace.

First, in the early years of the Internet (and to some extent today), the legal rules governing online dealings were unclear. In the late 1990s and early 2000s, legislative bodies throughout the world enacted laws to address the efficacy of electronic signatures, records, and privacy risks associated with electronic storage of personal information.[110] Likewise, the jurisdictional implications of online transactions were unclear.

Second, and perhaps more significantly, while the Internet and related technologies rapidly eliminated distance as an impediment to trade and collaboration, they did not eliminate impediments to dispute resolution. Courts do not hold trial in cyberspace nor (at least until recently) have neutrals been able to address disputes without in-person sessions or hearings—often involving considerable travel and scheduling expenses.

At present, there is a diverse range of dispute resolution services that fall within the rubric of Online Dispute Resolution or "ODR," including automated negotiation systems, facilitated negotiation and brainstorming, and, of course, online mediation and arbitration. Presently, most ODR systems are directed at resolving routine consumer or financial disputes in which the cost of "in-person" dispute resolution might far outweigh the amounts in dispute. Indeed, for many ecommerce transactions—such as trades on eBay or online consumer orders—in the absence of ODR systems, there might not be any economically viable means for resolving disputes.

Even sophisticated disputes may benefit from ODR, however. ODR can avoid costly travel and related settlement expenses and provide a means to continue and persist in settlement efforts when a single mediation session is inadequate.

---

[110] *See, generally,* (Kaplan G. L., The emerging law of information technology—Acquisition, Implementation, Dispute Resolution, 2000); (Kaplan & Bernstein, 2000); (Kaplan G. L., Privacy Compliance Symposium—State, National, and International Requirements, 2001).

Automated Negotiation Systems

ODR includes automated negotiation in which the parties agree in advance to be bound by the terms of settlement established through the use of an information technology system. The parties, for example, may alternate between submitting settlement bids and allowing the system to split the difference once the proposals are within a specified range. Alternatively, the system may split the surplus in circumstances in which an offer is greater than the amount the opposing party has indicated it will accept.

Notwithstanding the simplicity of a "split the difference" algorithm, automated negotiation systems have proven well suited and efficient alternatives for a wide range of disputes—especially those involving straight-forward matters, such as collection of consumer debts, routine insurance claims, parking tickets, etc.

For example, CyberSettle.com offers an automated negotiation service that allows each side to enter three successive offers. When a demand is less than an offer, the case settles at the median amount. CyberSettle offers the following example:[111]

Once [a participant] logs in he or she will have 3 opportunities (rounds) to settle the claim. One demand or offer is entered for each round. Each round, CyberSettle instantly compares the demands to the opposition's corresponding offer. When the offer is greater than or equal to the opposition's demand, the claim instantly settles.

Round	Offer	Demand	Result
1	$10,000	$20,000	No Settlement
2	$12,000	$16,000	No Settlement
3	$14,000	$13,000	Settled for $13,500

If the case does not settle, the claim can be resubmitted or the parties can agree to participate in telephone facilitation services.

Since its inception in 1998, CyberSettle claims to have resolved 212,425 disputes having a total settlement value of $1,571,728,274. The success of CyberSettle and other automated systems confirms the psychological impediments that may hinder settlement through direct negotiation. In essence, the most significant service that CyberSettle provides is to eliminate "reactive devaluation"[112] as a barrier to settlement. Because the offers are blind and no

---

[111] http://www.cybersettle.com/info/products/claimresolution.aspx.

[112] *See* discussion above in Chapter V. In addition, blind bidding systems also eliminate potential

feedback is provided, participants cannot recalibrate their positions based upon the opposing parties' responses or treat the opposing parties' offer as a "sign of weakness," etc.

Facilitated Negotiation Systems

Facilitated negotiation systems refer to online forums that provide guidance and a vehicle for parties to discuss and resolve disputes on their own. Perhaps the most notable such system is the SquareTrade® program offered by eBay to resolve disputes between buyers and sellers.

Under the SquareTrade program, when a party initiates a claim, the software automatically emails the other party, informing them that a case has been filed and asking them what they are willing to do to resolve the dispute. If no settlement is reached by negotiation through the SquareTrade site, a party can ask for a mediator to become involved for a fee of $15.

Facilitated negotiation systems help bridge communications gap created by the anonymous nature of many online transactions. Many, if not most, online transactions are made by people who have never met and who may not even be identified to each other. Facilitated negotiation systems serve primarily to open lines of communication that might otherwise by costly or impossible to even to identify.

Online Arbitration

Again, some transactions might not be amenable to any means of recourse or dispute resolution in the absence of online systems. The complete absence of dispute resolution capabilities, however, might seriously undermine confidence in systems, such as eBay and Paypal, that allow for global transactions, and thereby limit their utility and growth.

If facilitated negotiation fails, the most efficient course may simply be to allow an agreed upon administrator to decide the matter. In many instances, online arbitration is both more efficient and preferred to online mediation because it avoids the expenses and time associated with shuttle diplomacy among multiple individuals.

Paypal, the global leader in transferring money between ecommerce sellers and consumers, has implemented its own online arbitration system to promote confidence in its ecommerce platform. Paypal provides a two-stage dispute resolution system for buyers and sellers. As with eBay's SquareTrade program,

---

disputes over the excess that may arise when one party is willing to pay more than the other party is willing to accept to settle the matter. In economic terms, this excess can be referred to as the settlement "surplus."

upon initiation of a claim, Paypal emails the opposing party and provides an online forum for the parties to attempt to resolve their dispute through negotiation. (In the interim, Paypal may freeze funds to assure availability upon resolution.) If those negotiations fail and a party escalates the matter, Paypal investigates and decides the matter based on information provided by the parties, including communications during the negotiation process. If, in the course of negotiations, the parties have identified acceptable settlement amounts, Paypal may impose a compromise settlement on the parties.[113]

Online Mediation

For complex disputes, online mediation may offer a far more cost-effective alternative than in-person meetings. In addition, online mediation may allow for negotiation over an extended period, which may be necessary to get over an impasse between the parties.

Online mediation can take several forms that take advantage of increasingly common technologies—instant messaging/chat room, email, and VoIP communications including video conferencing. In general, online mediation attempts to replicate in-person mediation protocols and includes areas for joint discussions and appropriate protections for confidentiality in each instance. Significantly, though, online mediation permits sessions to be conducted in real time (*i.e.*, synchronously) or over extended periods in which the parties and mediators exchange messages seriatim as their individual schedules and analyses permit.

Although online mediation can be conducted through exchanges and email and the like, it is often advantageous to make use of a mediation platform in which the parties and a mediator post messages to a bulletin board system. Such systems include a common area visible to all participants and caucus areas visible to only the mediator and the respective parties.

In comparison with traditional mediation, online mediation offers several potential benefits. Most obviously, it eliminates travel and meeting costs. In addition, to the extent it requires written rather than verbal communication, online mediation may encourage greater reflection and consideration of alternatives for resolving the dispute.

On the other hand, the absence of gestures and physical clues may make it difficult to establish trust and rapport among the parties and mediators. Further, delays in communication may prevent the negotiations from achieving

---

[113] The details of Paypal's program can be found in its User Agreement, which is available at https://www.paypal.com/us/cgi-bin/webscr?cmd=xpt/UserAgreement/ua/USUA#spp-policy. (Paypal).

momentum toward settlement. In addition, poorly crafted email messages may unintentionally convey hostile sentiments or otherwise derail progress. Lastly, by reducing the cost of—or investment in—the mediation process, the savings from meeting online, rather than in person, may have the unintended effect of reducing the likelihood of settlement.[114]

In many cases, the optimal approach to mediation may include both traditional face-to-face meetings and access to online tools. In effect, the online forum can serve as a case management tool and diary for the parties and the mediator. In advance of in-person mediation, the online forum may be used to exchange background information and to establish ground rules for the mediation. If progress is made during a mediation session but settlement is not achieved, the online forum may be used to record any interim agreements. After the initial session, the online forum may be used to continue discussions and preparation for follow-up sessions, which may be conducted either in-person or through online text or video conferences.

The Future: ADR in Virtual Worlds

In April 2007, Business Week reported:

> Over the past year, Intel employees from Singapore, Israel, and the U.S. have convened via high-level computerized conferences, collaborating on such projects as product strategy and information-technology planning. But these are no ordinary online meetings. They've happened in virtual worlds, with three-dimensional graphic characters, or avatars, standing in for actual Intel (INTC) employees, making notes, holding conversations, and solving problems.

*   *   *

> At the typical global corporation, 20% of employees have never met their boss in person ... And 3D spaces offer a level of interaction that's not possible over the phone or via videoconferencing, says Sebastien Jeanjean, head of sales and marketing at France's Tixeo, a maker of corporate virtual-world software used by customers including Raytheon. "In 2D, even if you hear and see a person, you still have a feeling of being alone," Jeanjean says. "After half an hour, it's very difficult to keep people's attention." But

---

[114] Although the "sunk cost" fallacy can hinder settlement after parties have spent significant sums in litigation, it can promote settlement as a result of the parties' desire to avoid wasting their investment in the mediation process itself.

let users interact through avatars, and they will stay plenty engaged, the thinking goes. [115]

Background: A Brief Overview of Second Life® and Virtual Worlds.

Presently, Second Life®, a virtual world initiated and operated by Linden Research, Inc. (commonly called Linden Labs) is the most widely known 3-D environment accessible through the Internet. The Second Life world is accessible through a free computer program called the Second Life Viewer, which can be downloaded from the Second Life site at www.secondlife.com. The viewer allows users, called "Residents" of Second Life, to interact with each other through "avatars." Each resident is represented in the Second Life world by his or her avatar, which can walk, fly, teleport, communicate with others, and trade both virtual items (including land, building, clothing, etc.) and services.

The only way to fully understand Second Life (and other virtual worlds) and compare them to the now traditional world wide web is to try it. Screen shots tell only a small part of the story and the cartoonish appearance of many

avatars may be off-putting to serious-minded business executives. Nonetheless, in hopes of conveying a sense of virtual meeting, an example follows:[116]

Virtual worlds allow for a broad range of communications among users who may be dispersed around the world. In Second Life (commonly abbreviated SL), for example, there are two main methods of text-based communication: local chat and global "instant messaging" (known as IM). Chatting allows for

---

[115] (Karif, 2007).

[116] Courtesy of InWorldbusiness.com

conversations among multiple users (or avatars) who are in close proximity. Meanwhile, IM is used for private conversations, either between two avatars, among the members of a group, or even between objects and avatars. Unlike chatting, IM communication does not depend on the participants being within a certain distance of each other. In addition, IM communications can roll over into the users' non-SL email when he or she is logged off (if the avatar has opted into this service and has provided a valid email address.)

Second Life also allows for voice communications between or among users. Like text-based local chat, voice communications in SL can be spatially oriented—in other words, your avatar can speak to and listen to, avatars in close proximity. (In this mode, as in "real life," volume varies with distances). Second Life also allows for private one-on-one or group calls with other users. Alternatively, non-SL VoIP services, such as Skype, can be used simultaneously with SL to allow for verbal discussions. Voice communications can also be set to operate in a "push to talk" mode—like a walkie-talkie—so that your conversation is muted unless you actively trigger talking to others.

A significant reason for the expansion (and popularity) of Second Life is that much of the world's content—including avatars, buildings, cities, etc.—are developed by the users/Residents themselves. User-generated content comprises a large portion of the activity within Second Life. The SL Viewer includes a modeling tool that allows any Resident to build virtual objects, and they can also create gestures, animations, and scripts. Content created by users can range from simple clothing and furniture to complete virtual (and autonomous) ecology systems.

The other notable feature of Second Life is that it operates its own virtual economy with currency (Linden $) that can be converted in real currency. Although the exchange rate for Linden$ fluctuates a bit, it commonly ranges between $260L and $270L per U.S. Dollar.

Notwithstanding significant press attention and notable experiments, virtual worlds are in their infancy. Like the early days of the Internet, the space is populated primarily with "early adopters" who are comfortable with new technologies. Nonetheless, there have been notable projects and events that reveal the potential of virtual worlds for business applications, education, collaboration, and dispute resolution.

For example, IBM held a multiday virtual event in Second Life, in which Sam Palmisano, their CEO, spoke from a re-creation of the Forbidden City in Beijing. Cisco is also reported to be a heavy user of Second Life.[117]

---

[117] (Pattiso, 2008).

Numerous universities have established a "campus" in SL including the University of Queensland, Princeton University, Rice University, Vassar College, Harvard, INSEAD, Pepperdine, University of North Carolina at Chapel Hill, New York University, Ithaca College, University of Houston, Case Western Reserve University, and Stanford.

In early 2007, the New York Times reported:

Scores of colleges and universities have set up campuses on islands, where classes meet and students interact in real time. They can hold chat discussions and create multimedia presentations from virtual building blocks called prims. The laws of physics don't necessarily apply.

*   *   *

Instructors say the Second Life class experience is particularly enhanced for distance learners. In Second Life, classmates and instructor don't just communicate in chat rooms; they can actually see one another — or, at least, digital alter egos — on screen.

*   *   *

Rebecca Nesson, a Ph.D. candidate in computer science, brought her class at Harvard Extension School to Second Life last semester. "Normally, no matter how good a distance-learning class is, an inherent distance does still exist between you and your students," she says. "Second Life has really bridged that gap. There is just more unofficial time that we spend together outside of the typical class session."[118]

Second Life has also provided a forum and created communities and locales for virtual diplomacy. Three countries—the Maldives, Sweden and Estonia—have opened embassies.[119]

Second Life is not alone in developing technology to allow for virtual meetings, collaboration, trade shows, and the like. Firms including Qwaq, Tixeo, and Forterra Systems have developed environments and services for business collaboration, education, and other implementations.

---

[118] (Lagorio, 2007).

[119] *See* http://www.diplomacy.edu/DiplomacyIsland/default.asp

ADR in Virtual Sessions

Personal contact remains the gold standard for mediation, arbitration hearings, and collaboration. In the past 25 years, conference call (including video conferencing) technologies have become inexpensive and pervasive. Nonetheless, in the absence of cost and/or travel constraints, experience suggests that remote meetings via such technologies remain a poor substitute for personal meetings when attempting to promote settlement or decide disputes. For these reasons, most courts that require ADR as part of their standard procedures, or that conduct settlement conferences in advance of trial, require a representative of each party with settlement authority to attend in person. Many courts require insurers' representatives to attend also.

The unanswered question, then, is whether virtual sessions with 3-D avatars provide a richer and more fruitful environment for dispute resolution than more common technology. Because virtual worlds are plainly in their infancy, it may be some time before a clear answer emerges.

Currently, some obvious impediments exist to widespread acceptance and participation in virtual worlds for business functions. First, Second Life and other virtual world technologies require a fair degree of IT sophistication. Although Second Life and comparable systems are, quite literally, a walk in the park for gamers and individuals with a high level of comfort with IT systems, they are not yet intuitive for many. Over time, virtual worlds will inevitably become more "user friendly" while, at the same, public comfort levels with technologies will continue to increase.

Second, serious business executive may be put off by both cartoonish avatars and the game-like ambience of virtual worlds. This too may change over time. Avatars will doubtless become more realistic as technology and bandwidth continue to improve. As serious businesses continue to take footholds in virtual worlds, the gaming/cartoon stigma will erode.

Third, concerns about confidentiality and the security of confidential information in virtual worlds need to be addressed. Confidentiality is the hallmark of ADR and any significant implementation of ADR in virtual worlds needs provide appropriate protections.

Notwithstanding such reasonable grounds for pessimism (or even cynicism) about ADR in virtual sessions, there is also much reason for interest and optimism.

First, even in the absence of a formal study on the differences between a virtual world conference—or virtual session—and video conferencing, conferences in 3-D virtual worlds are simply more engaging than two-dimensional videoconferences. Proponents of virtual worlds describe the technology as "immersive."

One widely cited explanation for why 3-D immersive technologies are more effective for learning and collaboration than flat technology rests on the nature of learning itself. In particular, first-person experiences may be essential to, or at least enhance, effective learning. In his 1993 paper, "A Conceptual Basis for Educational Applications of Virtual Reality,"[120] Winn explains that immersive 3-D technologies, such as virtual reality tools developed by the Air Force to enable pilots to interact with flight data, are characterized by the seeming elimination of an artificial interface. In a "super cockpit," the pilot can operate some of the aircraft's controls by performing natural actions, such as looking, pointing, and touching. Likewise, an immersive learning environment is one in which the barrier between the student and subject matter, *e.g.*, the computer interface, is sufficiently unobtrusive as to enable the student to experience the subject matter first hand, rather than third hand (such as through a description in a book or lecture).

The challenge (and promise) of virtual worlds is to create environments that feel, and allow for interactions, more akin to first-hand experiences than remote ones. Winn explains:

> First-person experiences are ... natural, non-reflective, private, and predominate in our everyday interactions with the world. On this view, interacting with a computer through an interface is a third person experience. Even though we may master the keyboard or mouse to a level of skill where we use them automatically, the information the machine presents always requires reflection before we respond to it, is always objective, usually comes from someone other than ourselves, and precludes interactivity on the basis of natural behavior. We experience the computer as an object "out there" in the world. The information it gives us is contained in it and is not directly accessible. It is for this reason that software designers are frequently concerned, first and foremost, about our mental model of the system projected by the interface ... and only then with the functionality of the program. The interface creates a boundary around the computer and its information, and establishes the distinction between us – "subject" – and it – "object." In short, it defies first-person experiences.

---

[120] (Winn, 1993).

... [I]mmersion in a virtual world effectively removes the interface allowing us to cross the subject-object boundary that exists between us and the machine. Once this has happened, our experiences in the virtual world can be of exactly the same quality as our experiences in the real world. The knowledge they engender is direct, personal, subjective and often tacit, in other words first person. Immersive [technology] allows us to create from our experiences the kind of knowledge that has hitherto been accessible only through direct experience of the world.

To add credence to the theoretical underpinnings of virtual worlds (and the experiences they provide), researchers have begun measuring physiological responses to social interactions in virtual environments. In one study, for example, physiological responses (as measured by electrocardiogram and galvanic skin responses) of subjects were measured during social interactions in a virtual bar.[121] Another article suggests that although verbal and visual communications play important roles in both the real and virtual worlds in creating a sense of "togetherness," "perhaps the channel with the greatest potential for enhancing the sense of togetherness in shared virtual worlds is the tactile channel."[122] In other words, the ability to touch objects, or even virtual objects, may trigger a sense of togetherness, because unlike sight and hearing, in the real world, "[t]ouch is not ... a 'distance sense,' since one must be very close to an object in order to be able to touch it."[123]

Although such research, like virtual worlds, is in an early stage, it demonstrates that progress that has been made, and will inevitably continue to be made, in creating first-person experiences in virtual worlds. For ADR, and especially mediation, advances in creating first-person experiences may ultimately improve the degree to which conferences at a distance (through virtual session) may better replicate the circumstances of in-person meetings that permit participants to develop the trust and rapport often needed for effective negotiation and dispute resolution.

Even today, virtual worlds like Second Life allow for greater realism, in some respects, than videoconferencing. Although avatars in virtual worlds do not readily allow the parties to read each other's faces and body language, important components of communication (and which can be conveyed to a limited extent through video conference), they allow for other aspects that may offset the missing visual clues.

---

[121] (Slater, 2006).
[122] (Durlach, 2000).
[123] Ibid.

Thus, although they may not see each other's facial expressions, participants in a virtual conference can see each other sitting together at (a virtual) conference table, can share objects (such as diagrams or other text), and can "walk" to separate conference rooms for caucusing. Whether such capabilities do a better job of triggering a psychological sense of presence or togetherness than telephone or videoconferences has yet to be established. Indeed, it may be the case that different modes of creating virtual meetings for the purpose of mediation and ADR will work best for different groups of individuals or subject matter.

Efficient dispute resolution is not subject to a one-size-fits-all solution. On the other hand, it is patently clear that traditional litigation seldom is the best, and most efficient, fit for business disputes. Even in the absence of sophisticated technology, alternatives such as mediation, arbitration, and investigatory arbitration, have the potential to save extraordinary sums while providing higher-quality decisions and solutions than often result from litigation. Advances in IT serve not only to enhance the efficiency of traditional dispute resolution alternatives but also to expand the range of alternatives that may be available to manage business disputes most efficiently.

CHAPTER XII: Conclusion

Although the use of ADR has grown dramatically in the past 20 years, dependence on costly, inefficient litigation remains the rule rather than the exception. Why should executives care about dispute management?

First, as we have seen, litigation is a perfect storm of circumstances that leads parties to make bad decisions. Research in negotiation theory, behavioral economics, decision science, and psychology shows that inherent human biases invariably lead parties to overstate the value or strength of their claims or defenses and underestimate the cost and burden of litigation.

Second, from a purely economic standpoint, and when considered as a decision-making process, litigation is woefully inefficient for resolving disputes. The process requires each side to engage in multiple iterations of redundant (and costly) tasks to seek a decision by a judge or jury who may have little if any experience with the subject of the dispute. In the end, there may be little correlation between the cost of the dispute and the quality of the resulting determination.

Third, when properly implemented, ADR—especially mediation—is more likely to achieve an efficient resolution because it can address (and neutralize) the inherent human biases and strategic incentives that impede timely settlements. For example, shuttle diplomacy can resolve disputes in circumstances in which direct talks would fail. As shown in Chapter VII, two innovative approaches to dispute resolution could directly address the inefficiencies of traditional litigation: (i) Investigatory Mediation and Arbitration, which would focus on eliminating redundancies while promoting high-quality decision making by an invested and qualified neutral, and (ii) Co-expert Mediation which would marry two critical, but often missing, elements for effective mediation—dispute resolution expertise and subject matter expertise.

Finally, disputes are entirely predictable and a modicum of planning can dramatically reduce the costs and improve the quality of resolution. By considering and applying principles of ADR and sound economic logic, most modern businesses, nonprofit organizations, and healthcare providers have the opportunity not only to save extraordinary expense but also to preserve and engender the positive relationships, both internal and external, upon which they must invariably depend.

Works Cited

Adams, M. (2000, September 8). CEOs Now Love to Say "Sorry." *USA Today*, p. 3B.

Air Force Instruction 36-1201. (2007, February 12). Retrieved from http://www.adr.af.mil/shared/media/document/AFD-070402-075.pdf.

American Arbitration Association. (n.d.). *Commercial Arbitration Rules and Mediation Procedure*. Retrieved September 1, 2008, from American Arbitration Association: http://www.adr.org/sp.asp?id-22440.

American Bar Association, Section of Dispute Resolution. (2008). *Final Report: Task Force on Improving Mediation Quality*. Washington, D.C.: American Bar Association.

Arkes, H., & Blumer, C. (1985). The Psychology of Sunk Cost. *Organizational Behavior and Human Decision Process, 35*, 124–140.

Arkes, H., & Hutzel, L. (2000). The Role of Probability of Success Estimates in the Sunk Cost Effect. *Journal of Behavioural Decision Making*, 295–306.

Armor, D. A., & Taylor, S. E. (2002). When Predictions Fail: The Dilemma of Unrealistic Optimism. In T. Gilovich, D. W. Griffin, & D. Kahneman, *Heuristics and Biases: The Psychology of Intuitive Judgment* (p. 334). Cambridge University Press.

Armstrong, P. M. (1998). CASE Study: Georgia Pacific's Aggressive Use of Early Case Evaluation and ADR. *ACCA Docket, 16* (6), 42–48.

Armstrong, P.M. (1999, December), Axing Arbitration, *Corporate Counsel*.

Armstrong, P. M. (2005, May). Georgia Pacific's ADR Program: A Critical Review After 10 Years. *Dispute Resolution Journal*.

Atwood, D. (2008, April 1). Impact of Medical Apology Statutes and Policies. *Journal of Nursing Law, 12*, 43–53.

Axelrod, R. (1984). *The Evolution of Cooperation*. New York: Basic Books.

Babcock, L., & Loewenstein, G. Explaining Bargaining Impasse: The Role of Self-Serving Biases. *Journal of Economic Perspectives, 11*, 109–126.

Bedman, W. L. (n.d.). Retrieved September 4, 2008, from http://www.mediate.com/articles/bedmanW.cfm.

Berwick, D. M. (2003). Disseminating Innovations in Health Care. *Journal of the American Medical Association, 280* (15).

Birke, R., & Fox, C. R. (1999). Psychological Principles in Negotiating Civil Settlements. *Harv. Negotiation L. Rev., 4* (1), 16–17.

Brown, H. (1997). Alternative Dispute Resolution Realities and Remedies. *Suffolk U.L. Rev., 30*, 743.

Carr, C. A., & Jencks, M. R. (1999). The Privatization of Business and Commercial Dispute Resolution. *Ky. L. Jour., 88* (2), 183–243.

Carwardine, R. (2006). *Lincoln: A Life of Purpose and Power*. Alfred A. Knopf.

Clinton, H. J., & Obama, B. (2006). Making Patient Safety the Centerpiece of Medical Liability Reform. *New England Journal of Medicine, 354* (21).

Coase, R. (1960). The Problem of Social Cost. *Journal of Law and Economics, 3* (1), 1.

Cooley, J. (2002, February). A Dose of ADR for the Health Care Industry. *Dispute Resolution Journal.*

CPR Institute for Dispute Resolution. (2002). In *How Companies Manage Employment Disputes: A Compendium of Leading Employment Programs.*

Craver, C.B. (2005). Effective Legal Negotiation and Settlement, Fifth Edition. Mathew Bender.

Cross, P. (1999). Not Can, but Will Teaching be Improved? *New Directions for Higher Education, 17,* 1.

Durlach, N. (2000). Presence in Shared Virtual Environments and Virtual Togetherness. *Presence, 9* (2), 214–217.

Gilson, R. J. (2000). Cooperation and Competition Litigation: Can Lawyers Dampen Conflict? *Barriers to Conflict Resolution.*

Glater, J. D. (2008, August 8). Study Finds Settling is Better than Going to Trial. *New York Times,* p. (online edition).

Gross, D. J., & Charles, W. F. (2003). *PTM: The Power Trial Method.* National Institutes of Trial Advocacy, Inc.

Gross, S., & Syverud, K. (1996). Don't Try, Civil Jury Verdicts in a System Geared to Settlement. *UCLA Law Review,* 44, 51.

Guadagnino, C. (2004, April). Malpractice and Mediation Poised to Expand. *Physician's News Digest.*

Haidt, J. (2006). *The Happiness Hypothesis.* Basic Books.

Hastorf, A. T., & Cantril, H. (1954). They Saw a Game: A Case Study. *Journal of Abnormal and Social Psychology, 49* (1), 129–134.

Jonakait, R. N. (2006). *The American Jury System.* Yale University Press.

Jones, E. E., & Harris, V. A. (1967). The Attribution of Attitudes. *Journal of Experimental Social Psychology, 3,* 1–24.

Kahneman, D., & Tversky, A. (1982). Subjective Probability: A Judgment of Representativeness. In D. Kahneman, P. Slovic, & A. Tversky, *Judgment Bias Under Uncertainty: Heuristics and Biases.* New York: Cambridge University Press.

Kalven Jr., H., & Zeisel, H. (1966). *The American Jury.* Little, Brown.

Kaplan, G. L. (2000, April 4). The Emerging Law of Information Technology–Acquisition, Implementation, Dispute Resolution. *Pennsylvania Bar Quarterly.*

Kaplan, G. L. (2001, April). Privacy Compliance Symposium–State, National, and International Requirements. *Pennsylvania Bar Quarterly.*

Kaplan, G. L., & Bernstein, L. (2000, October). Electronic Signatures in Global and National Commerce Act. *The National Law Journal.*

Karif, O. (2007, April 16). The Virtual Meeting Room. *Business Week,* online edition.

Kidwell, R.P. & Voinchet, R. (2008, June). Mediation of Medical Professional Liability Claims. *Hospitals and Health Systems Rx,* 10(2), 5-7.

Knox, R., & Inkster, J. A. (1969). Postdecision Dissonance at Post Tim. *Journal of Personality and Social Psychology, 8* (4), 319–323.

Lagorio. (2007, January 7). The Ultimate Distance Learning. *New York Times*, online edition.

Larson, E. (1989). Innovations in Health Care: Antisepsis as a Case Study. *American Journal of Public Health*, 92-99.

Leibman, C., & Hyman, C. (2004). A Mediation Skills Model to Manage Disclosure of Errors and Adverse Events to Patients. *Health Affairs, 23* (4), 22–32.

Lipsky, D. B., & Seeber, R. L. (1998). In Search for Control: The Corporate Embrace of ADR. *Univ. of Pennsylvania Journal of Labor and Employment Law, 1*, 133–157.

Lipsky, D. B., & Seeber, R. L. (2003). *Emerging Systems for Managing Workplace Conflict.* Jossey Bass.

Loftus, E. F., & Wagenaar, W. A. (1988). Lawyers' Predictions of Success. *Jurimetrics, 28*, 437, 450.

Lord, C., Ross, L., & Lepper, M. R. (1979). Biased Assimilation and Attitude Polarization: The Effects of Prior Theories on Subsequently Considered Evidence. *Journal of Personality & Social Psychology, 37* (11), 2098–2109.

Malhotra, D., & Bazerman, M.H. (2007). *Negotiation Genius.* Bantam Books.

Mnookin, R., & Ross, L. (1995). Introduction. In K. Arrow, R. H. Mnookin, L. Ross, A. Tversky, & R. Wilson, *Barriers to Conflict Resolution* (pp. 1–24). New York: W.W. Norton & Co.

Patterson, K., Grenny, J., Maxfield, D., McMillan, R., & Switzer, A. (2008). *Influencer: The Power to Change Anything.* McGraw-Hill.

Pattiso, K. (2008, August 5). Why You should Have Your Next Meeting in Second Life. *Fast Company*, online edition.

Paypal. (n.d.). *User Agreement.* Retrieved September 4, 2008, from Paypal.com: https://www.paypal.com/us/cgi-bin/webscr?cmd=xpt/UserAgreement/ua/USUA#spp-policy.

Plous, S. (1991). Biases in the Assimilation of Technological Breakdowns: Do Accidents Make Us Safer? *Journal of Applied Social Psychology, 21* (13), 1058–1082.

Pound, R. (1906). The Causes of Popular Dissatisfaction with the Administration of Justice. *Given at the Annual Convention of the American Bar Ass'n.*

President Bush Announces Major Combat Operations in Iraq Have Ended. (2003, May 1). Retrieved October 29, 2008, from White House: http://www.whitehouse.gov/news/releases/2003/05/20030501-15.html.

Priest, G., & Klein, B. (1984). The Selection of Disputes for Litigation. *Journal of Legal Studies, 13* (1), 12.

Rachlinski, J. (1996). Gains, Losses, and the Psychology of Litigation. *S.Cal.L.Rev*, 113.

Rawls, J. (1971). *A Theory of Justice.* Belknap.

Refo, P. L. (2004, Winter). The Vanishing Trial. *Litigation: The Journal of the Section of Litigation, 30* (2), online edition.

Roberts, K. M., & Jessica, P. L. (2005). *Evaluative v. Facilitative Mediation in Complex Commercial Litigation*. Chicago, Illinois: American Bar Association, Section of Dispute Resolution, Tort Trial & Practice Section.

Rogers, E.M. (2003). *Diffusion of Innovations*. Free Press (Fifth Edition).

Rooney, J. F. (2008, July 8). An Early Resolution for Disputes. *Chicago Lawyer*.

Ross, L. (1977). The Intuitive Psychologist and His Shortcomings: Distortions in the Attribution Process. In L. Berkowitz, *Advances in Experimental Social Psychology* (Vol. 10, pp. 173–220). New York: Academic Press.

Sachs, S. E. (2006). From St. Ives to Cyberspace: The Modern Distortion of the Medieval Law Merchant. *Am. U. Int'l Law Rev., 21*, 685.

Sack, K. (2008, May 18). Doctors Say 'I'm Sorry' Before 'See You in Court. *New York Times*.

Seidman Diamond, S., Casper, J. D., Heiert, C. L., & Marshall, A.-M. (1996). Juror Reactions to Attorneys at Trial. *Journal of Criminal Law and Criminology, 87*.

Slaikeu, K. A. (1998). *Controlling the Costs of Conflict: How to Design a System for Your Organization*. Jossey Bass.

Slater, M. (2006). Analysis of Physiological Responses to Social Situation in an Immersive Virtual Environment. *Presence, 15* (5), 553–559.

Staw, B. (1976). Knee Deep in the Big Muddy. *Organizational Behavior and Human Decision Process*, 124–140.

The Maxwell School, Syracuse University. (n.d.). *Performance Measurement for ADR Professionals*. Retrieved from http://sites.maxwell.syr.edu/measuringADR/default.asp.

Thomson, D. B. (2001, Fall). A Disconnect of Supply and Demand: Survey of Forum Members' Mediation Preferences. *The Construction Lawyer*, pp. 17-22.

Tolstoy, L. (1893). The Kingdom of God is Within You-Chapter III.

Tolstoy, L. (1897). What is Art?

Transcript of Town Hall Meeting At Aviano Air Base. (2003, February 7). Retrieved October 29, 2008, from DefenseLink: http://www.defenselink.mil/transcripts/transcript.aspx?transcriptid=1900.

Trevarthen, D. S. (n.d.). Powerpoint Presentation: Toro's Alternative Dispute Resolution Program Handling Product Liability Claims and Lawsuits.

Tuchman, B. W. (1994). *The Guns of August*. New York: Ballantine Books.

Tversky, A., & Kahneman, D. (1974). Judgments Under Uncertainty: Heuristics and Biases. *Science, 185* (4157), 1124–1131.

Tyler, L. (1997). Liability Means Never Being Able to Say You're Sorry: Corporate Guilt, Legal Constraints, and Defensiveness in Corporate Communications. *Management Communication Quarterly, 11*, 51–73.

Ulen, T. S. (2006). Human Fallability and the Forms of Law: The Case of Traffic Safety. In F. Parisi, & V. L. Smith, *The Law and Economics of Irrational Behavior* (pp. 397, 410). Stanford University Press.

United States Air Force. (2002). *The Cost Savings Associated With The Air Force Alternative Dispute Resolution Program.* Retrieved September 4, 2008, from http://www.mediate.com/articles/airforceadr.cfm.

United States Air Force. (n.d.). *Sample Agreement.* Retrieved September 4, 2008, from http://www.adr.af.mil/factsheets/factsheet.asp?id=9935.

Vidmar, N., & Hans, V. P. (2007). *American Juries: The Verdict.* Prometheus Books.

Wason, P. C. (1960). On the Failure to Eliminate Hypotheses in a Conceptual Tack. *Quarterly Journal of Experimental Psychology, 12,* 129–140.

Weinstein, N. D. (1980). Unrealistic Optimism about Future Life Events. *Journal of Personality and Social Psychology, 39* (5).

Whyte, G. (1986). Escalating Commitment to a Course of Action: A Reinterpretation. *Academy of Management Review, 16,* 27–44.

Winn, W. (1993). *Report No. TR-93-9.* Human Interface Technology Laboratory, Washington Technology Center, University of Washington.

Yarn, D.H. (2000). The Attorney as Duelist's Friend: Lessons from the Code Duello. *Case Western Res. L. Rev.* 51(1), 69.

Index

Additional Praise for the
Executive Guide to Managing Disputes

"Gary Kaplan's book incisively addresses the broad range of disputes that can undermine business productivity. As consultants, we are often brought into the middle of conflicts between managers who have conducted their investigations, developed their grievances, and prepared to do battle in hopes of a favorable decision by senior executives who may be far removed from the facts. The costs of such internal battles can be as astonishing as in litigation. The *Executive Guide* both explains why business disputes often spiral out of control and provides sound guidance for managing such challenges. Thanks, Gary!"

~ David Sirota, Senior Managing Consultant, IBM Corporation

"Needless workplace disputes can hurt even the best run business by diverting attention and resources from productive uses. In the *Executive Guide*, Gary Kaplan clearly and thoughtfully explains how ADR can resolve isolated disputes through timely and meaningful intervention and prevent them from sparking costly chain reactions or even litigation."

~ Amy Cook, Director of Human Resources, Ariba, Inc.

"The Executive Guide is a superb introduction of Alternative Dispute Resolution (ADR) to business executives. It bridges the gap between academic theory and practical application, showing executives how ADR can be used in business settings to significantly reduce the cost of resolving a wide variety of disputes."

~ Richard Bales, Professor of Law, NKU/Chase Law School

Breinigsville, PA USA
05 January 2010
230100BV00001BA/4/P